RISE.
EXPAND.
EVOLVE.
ADAPT.

Mastering the Journey of Entrepreneurial Success.

Andrew Benham

Copyright © 2024 by Andrew Benham
All rights reserved.
No part of this publication may be reproduced, distributed, or transmitted in any form or by any means, including photocopying, recording, or other electronic or mechanical methods, without the prior written permission of the author, except in the case of brief quotations embodied in critical reviews and certain other noncommercial uses permitted by copyright law.

Table of Content

Chapter 1..4
The Spark of Innovation 4

Igniting Ideas 4
From Concept to Creation 4
Overcoming Inertia 4
Finding Your Why 4
Chapter 2 4
Laying the Foundation 4
Crafting a Vision 4
Setting Goals and Milestones 4
Building a Team 4
Defining Success Metrics 4
Chapter 3 4
Embracing Risk 4
Calculated Risks 4
Fear of Failure 4
Resilience and Adaptability 4
Learning from Setbacks 4
Chapter 4 4
Establishing a Brand 4
Brand Identity and Values 4
Brand Strategies 4
Positioning in the Market 4
Customer Engagement 4
Chapter 5 4
Scaling Operations 4
Operational Efficiency 4
Managing Growth 4
Technology Integration 4
Supply Chain Optimization 4
Chapter 6 4
Expanding Horizons 4
Market Expansion Strategies 4
International Growth 4
Strategic Partnership 4
Diversification 4
Chapter 7 4
Customer-Centric Approach 4
Understanding Customer Need 4
Building Customer Loyalty 4
Personalization and Customization 4

Feedback and Improvement 4
Chapter 8 4
Innovating for the Future 4
Continuous Innovation Culture 4
Disruptive Technology 4
R&D Investment 4
Future Trend Analysis 4
Chapter 9 4
Adapting to Change 4
Agility in a Dynamic Environment 4
Crisis Management 4
Leadership in Turbulent Times 4
Change Management Strategies 4
Chapter 10 4
Strategic Vision 4
Setting Long-term Goals 4
Visionary Leadership 4
Strategic Planning 4
Sustainable Growth Strategies 4
Chapter 11 4
Cultivating a Learning Culture 4
Learning Organizations 4
Employee Development Programs 4
Knowledge Sharing Initiatives 4
Continuous Training 4
Chapter 12 4
Mentoring and Coaching 4
Harnessing Mentorship 4
Coaching for Success 4
Peer Learning Groups 4
Leadership Development 4
Chapter 13 4
Embracing Failure 4
Learning from Mistakes 4
Fail Fast, Learn Faster 4
Cultivating Innovation through Failure 4
Resilience and Growth Mindset 4
Chapter 14 4
Knowledge Management 4

Capturing Organizational Knowledge 4
Knowledge Sharing Platforms 4
Intellectual Property Protection 4
Data-driven Decision making 4
Conclusion 4
Introduction 1

RISE

-
-
-
-
-

-
-
-
-
-

-
-
-
-
-

-
-
-
-
-

EXPAND

-
-
-
-

-
-
-
-
-
-

-
-
-
-

-
-
-
-

EVOLVE

-
-
-
-
-

-
-
-
-

ADAPT

-
-
-
-
-
-
-
-
-
-
-
-
-
-
-
-
-

Introduction

In the ever-evolving landscape of business, entrepreneurship stands as a beacon of innovation and boundless potential. Yet, the path to entrepreneurial success is not without its challenges. To be successful, you need to possess a rare combination of vision, resilience, and adaptability.

"Rise, Expand, Evolve, Adapt" is the definitive guide for aspiring and established entrepreneurs alike. This comprehensive roadmap provides a step-by-step framework for navigating the complexities of entrepreneurial ventures, from the initial spark of an idea to the ongoing pursuit of growth and success.

Through the lenses of "Rise, Expand, Evolve, and Adapt," you will:

- Rise: Discover the essential principles for launching a successful business, including market research, business planning, and funding strategies.
- Expand: Learn the art of scaling operations, building a strong team, and expanding your market reach.
- Evolve: Embrace innovation, adapt to changing conditions, and stay ahead of the competition.
- Adapt: Develop the resilience and adaptability necessary to overcome challenges, pivot when needed, and seize new opportunities.

This book is not merely a collection of theories but a practical guide filled with real-world examples, actionable advice, and inspiring stories from successful entrepreneurs. It is an indispensable resource for anyone who aspires to embark on or excel in the thrilling journey of entrepreneurship.

So, prepare to rise, expand, evolve, and adapt. The path to entrepreneurial success awaits you.

RISE

Chapter 1
The Spark of Innovation

Innovation is the process of coming up with new and improved methods of doing things, finding solutions to issues and satisfying wants. Innovation can be driven by various factors, such as curiosity, necessity, competition, or collaboration. However, behind every innovation, there is a spark that ignites the creative fire in the minds of the innovators. What is this spark, and how can we foster it?

The spark of innovation is the moment when an idea, a question, or a challenge emerges in the consciousness of an individual or a group. It is the initial inspiration that motivates one to pursue a novel solution, a new perspective, or a different approach. The spark of innovation can come from various sources, such as:

- **Observation:** By paying attention to the world around us, we can notice gaps, inefficiencies, or opportunities for improvement. For example, the invention of the microscope was sparked by the observation of tiny organisms in a drop of water.

- **Experimentation:** By trying out different things, we can discover new possibilities, test hypotheses, or learn from failures. For example, the discovery of penicillin was sparked by the accidental contamination of a bacterial culture by mold.

- **Imagination:** By using our creativity, we can envision scenarios, alternatives, or solutions that do not exist yet. For example, the creation of the Harry Potter series was sparked by the imagination of a young writer on a train ride.

- **Connection:** By interacting with others, we can exchange ideas, feedback, or perspectives that can enrich our own thinking. For example, the development of the World Wide Web was sparked by the collaboration of a team of computer scientists.

The spark of innovation is not a rare or random occurrence, but a potential that exists in everyone. However, to ignite and sustain it, we need to cultivate certain conditions, such as:

- **Curiosity:** By being curious, we can keep our minds open, explore new domains, and ask questions that challenge the status quo.

- **Passion:** By being passionate, we can find meaning, motivation, and joy in our work, and overcome obstacles and setbacks.
- **Courage:** By being courageous, we can take risks, embrace uncertainty, and face criticism or rejection.

- **Persistence:** By being persistent, we can follow through, refine, and improve our ideas, and learn from feedback or failure.

The spark of innovation is the starting point of a journey that can lead to remarkable outcomes, such as new products, services, processes, or art forms. However, the spark alone is not enough. We also need to nurture it with the fuel of knowledge, skills, resources, and support. By doing so, we can unleash our creative potential and contribute to the advancement of humanity.

Igniting Ideas

Have you ever wondered how some people come up with brilliant ideas that change the world? Whether it is a scientific discovery, a technological innovation, or a creative masterpiece, these ideas often seem to emerge out of nowhere. However, behind every great idea, there is a process of igniting, nurturing, and developing it.

Igniting ideas is the process of generating and developing creative and innovative solutions to various problems or challenges. It is a crucial skill for individuals and organizations in the 21st century, as it enables them to adapt to changing circumstances, overcome obstacles, and create value for themselves and others. In this section, I will discuss the importance of igniting ideas, the factors that influence it, and the strategies that can enhance it.

One of the reasons why igniting ideas is important is that it can lead to social and economic benefits. By generating and implementing new ideas, individuals and organizations can create products, services, or processes that meet the needs and wants of customers, users, or beneficiaries. This can result in increased satisfaction, loyalty, and revenue, as well as improved efficiency, quality, and sustainability. For instance, Apple is a company that is known for its ability to ignite ideas and create innovative and user-friendly devices, such as the iPhone, the iPad, and the MacBook. These products have revolutionized the fields of communication, entertainment, and education, and have made Apple one of the most valuable and influential companies in the world.

However, igniting ideas is not always easy or straightforward. There are many factors that can affect the generation and development of ideas, such as personal traits, environmental conditions, and social influences. Some of these factors can facilitate the process, while others can hinder it. For example, some personal traits that can foster igniting ideas are curiosity, openness, and risk-taking, as they enable people to explore new possibilities, embrace different perspectives, and experiment with various options. On the other hand, some environmental conditions that can inhibit igniting ideas are stress, time pressure, and lack of resources, as they can limit people's attention, motivation, and creativity.

Igniting ideas is a vital skill for the modern world, as it can generate positive outcomes for individuals and organizations, as well as for society at large. However, igniting ideas is also influenced by various factors, both internal and external, that can either enhance or impair the process. Therefore, it is important to understand and apply the strategies that can help to ignite ideas, such as brainstorming, collaborating, and prototyping. By doing so, we can unleash our potential and make a difference in the world.

From Concept to Creation

Innovation is the process of transforming an idea into a valuable product, service, or solution. Innovation can be driven by various factors, such as customer needs, market opportunities, technological advances, or social challenges. Innovation, on the other hand, is not a process that can be described as linear or predictable. It involves multiple stages of exploration, experimentation, evaluation, and execution. In this section, I will describe the main steps of the innovation process, from concept to creation.

- The first step of the innovation process is to generate a concept. A concept is a general idea or vision of what the innovation aims to achieve or solve. A concept can be inspired by different sources, such as existing problems, customer feedback, competitor analysis, or creative thinking. A concept should be clear, concise, and compelling, as it serves as the foundation for the subsequent steps.

- The second step of the innovation process is to develop a prototype. A prototype is a tangible representation of the concept, such as a sketch, a model, a mock-up, or a simulation. A prototype allows the innovator to test and refine the concept, as well as to communicate and demonstrate it to potential users, customers, or stakeholders. A prototype should be simple, functional, and iterative, as it enables the innovator to learn and improve the concept.

- The third step of the innovation process is to validate the prototype. Validation is the process of gathering feedback and data from the target market or audience, to assess the feasibility, desirability, and viability of the prototype. Validation can be done through various methods, such as surveys, interviews, focus groups, or experiments. Validation should be objective, reliable, and relevant, as it helps the innovator to measure and optimize the value proposition of the prototype.

- The final step of the innovation process is to launch the product. A product is the final outcome of the innovation process, which is ready to be delivered and distributed to the market or society. A product should be scalable, sustainable, and adaptable, as it needs to meet the changing needs and expectations of the customers or users. A product should also be distinctive, competitive, and impactful, as it aims to create a positive difference in the world.

The innovation process is a complex and dynamic journey, that requires creativity, experimentation, feedback, and execution. By following the four steps of the innovation process, from concept to creation, an innovator can turn an idea into a reality and make a meaningful contribution to the society or the economy.

Overcoming Inertia

The propensity of an item to exhibit resistance to a change in its state of motion is referred to as inertia. It is also a metaphor for the human tendency to resist a change in our habits, behaviors, and actions. Inertia can be a powerful force that keeps us stuck in the status quo, preventing us from pursuing our goals and dreams.

However, inertia is not an unsurmountable obstacle. There are strategies and techniques that can help us overcome inertia and get moving in the direction of our desired outcomes. In this section, I will discuss three of these strategies: creating a compelling vision, breaking down the goal into manageable steps, and finding accountability and support.

One of the reasons why we may experience inertia is that we lack a clear and compelling vision of what we want to achieve. Without a vision, we may not have a strong motivation to change our current situation, or we may not know where to start or what to do. A vision is a vivid and detailed picture of our desired future state, that inspires us and guides our actions. A vision can help us overcome inertia by:

- Providing us with a purpose and a direction for our efforts.

- Generating positive emotions and excitement that fuel our motivation.

- Helping us overcome fear and doubt by focusing on the benefits and possibilities of our goal.

- Enabling us to measure our progress and celebrate our achievements.

To create a compelling vision, we can use techniques such as visualization, affirmations, journaling, or vision boards. We can also use questions such as:

- What are my goals and why do I want to accomplish them?

- How will I feel when I achieve it?

- How does it sound and how does it even feel?

- What are the benefits and rewards of achieving it?

- What are the challenges and risks of not achieving it?

Breaking Down the Goal into Manageable Steps

Another reason why we may experience inertia is that we feel overwhelmed by the size or complexity of our goal. We may not have a clear plan of action, or we may not have the skills, resources, or confidence to tackle the goal. This can lead to procrastination, avoidance, or paralysis. To overcome this, we can break down the goal into manageable steps, which are:

- Specific: They define what, when, where, and how we will do something.

- Measurable: They have a clear criterion or indicator of completion or success.

- Achievable: They are realistic and within our reach, given our current situation and abilities.

- Relevant: They are aligned with our vision and values, and contribute to our overall goal.

- -Time-bound: They have a deadline or a timeframe for completion.

By breaking down the goal into manageable steps, we can overcome inertia by:

- Reducing the complexity and ambiguity of the goal, and making it more clear and concrete.

- Increasing our sense of control and confidence, by focusing on what we can do and what we have.

- Creating a roadmap and a sequence of actions that guide our behavior and decision making.

- Building momentum and motivation, by achieving quick wins and seeing the results of our efforts.

To break down the goal into manageable steps, we can use tools such as SMART goals, action plans, checklists, or calendars. We can also use questions such as:

- What are the main components or sub-goals of my goal?

- What are the actions or tasks that I need to do to achieve each sub-goal?

- How can I prioritize and sequence the actions or tasks?

- How will I know that I have completed each action or task.
- When will I do each action or task?

The third reason why we may experience inertia is that we lack accountability and support for our goal. We may not have anyone to hold us responsible for our actions, or to provide us with feedback, guidance, or encouragement. We may also face resistance or criticism from others who do not share or understand our vision. This can lead to isolation, discouragement, or distraction. To overcome this, we can find accountability and support for our goal by:

- Sharing our vision and goal with someone who can act as a coach, mentor, or partner, and who can help us monitor our progress, evaluate our performance, and celebrate our successes.

- Joining a group or a community of people who have similar or related goals, and who can offer us advice, inspiration, or collaboration.

- Seeking out role models or examples of people who have achieved or are working towards our goal, and who can show us the possibilities and the best practices.

- Asking for help or feedback from others who have the skills, knowledge, or resources that we need or lack.

- Avoiding or minimizing contact with people who are negative, unsupportive, or discouraging of our goal.

By finding accountability and support for our goal, we can overcome inertia by:

- Increasing our commitment and responsibility for our actions, and reducing the temptation to quit or give up.

- Enhancing our learning and improvement, by receiving constructive feedback and suggestions.

- Boosting our morale and confidence, by receiving praise and recognition.

- Expanding our network and resources, by connecting with others who can help us or benefit from our goal.

- Protecting our vision and goal, by distancing ourselves from people who can harm or hinder us.

Inertia is a common challenge that can prevent us from achieving our goals and dreams. However, it is not impossible to overcome. By creating a compelling vision, breaking down the goal into manageable steps, and finding accountability and support, we can break free from the status quo and get moving in the direction of our desired outcomes. The key is to just start, and keep going, until we reach our destination.

Finding Your Why

Finding your why is the process of discovering your purpose in life and aligning it with your actions. It is a powerful way to achieve personal and professional fulfillment, as well as to make a positive impact on the world. I will explain what finding your why means, why it is important, and how you can find your own why.

What is finding your why?

Finding your why is based on the idea that everyone has a unique reason for being, a core motivation that drives their choices and behaviors. This reason is often hidden or obscured by external factors, such as social expectations, cultural norms, or personal fears. However, when you uncover your why, you gain clarity on what matters most to you, what you are passionate about, and what you want to contribute to the world.

Finding your why is not the same as finding your goals, your career, or your hobbies. These are expressions of your why, but they are not the essence of it. Your why is deeper and more enduring than any specific outcome or activity. It is the underlying theme that connects all aspects of your life and gives them meaning.

Why is finding your why important?

Firstly, it helps you live authentically and intentionally. When you know your why, you can align your actions with your values and principles, and avoid wasting time and energy on things that are not aligned with your purpose. You can also make better decisions, as you have a clear criterion to evaluate your options and prioritize what is important.

Secondly, finding your why boosts your motivation and performance. When you are passionate about what you do, you are more likely to overcome challenges, persist in the face of difficulties, and achieve your goals. You also experience more joy and satisfaction, as you are doing something that fulfills you and makes you happy.

Thirdly, finding your why inspires others and creates positive change. When you share your why with the world, you can influence people with your vision and values, and inspire them to join your cause or find their own why. You can also make a difference in the world, as you are contributing your unique gifts and talents to a greater purpose.

How can you find your own why?

Finding your own why is a personal and introspective journey that requires time, effort, and courage. There is no one-size-fits-all formula, but there are some steps that can guide you along the way. Here are some suggestions:

Reflect on your past experiences and identify the moments when you felt most alive, fulfilled, and proud. What were you doing? Who were you with? What impact did you have?
Analyze your strengths and passions and discover what you are good at and what you enjoy doing. What skills and talents do

you have? What are the hobbies that cause you to lose track of time? What topics or issues excite you?

Ask yourself why you do what you do and what is the ultimate goal or outcome that you seek. Why do you care about your work, your hobbies, your relationships, or your causes? What is the value or benefit that you provide or receive?

Synthesize your findings and craft a concise and compelling statement that summarizes your why. Use simple and clear language that expresses your core motivation and purpose. For example, "I help people find their voice and express themselves creatively" or "I create innovative solutions that improve people's lives".

Test and refine your why statement and see if it resonates with you and others. Ask for feedback from people who know you well and who share your values. Check if your statement is authentic, inspiring, and actionable. If not, revise it until it feels right.

Live your why and integrate it into your daily life. Use your why statement as a guide and a reminder for your actions and decisions. Seek opportunities that align with your why and avoid those that do not. Communicate your why to others and invite them to support you or join you.

Finding your why is a rewarding and transformative process that can help you live a more meaningful and fulfilling life. It can also help you make a positive difference in the world and inspire others to do the same. I encourage you to find your own why and share it with the world

Chapter 2
Laying the Foundation

Laying the foundation is a phrase that means to provide the basic ideas or structures from which something much larger develops. It can be used in various contexts, such as engineering, education, science, business, and politics. In this section, I will explain the meaning and importance of laying the foundation in different domains, and give some examples of how it can be done effectively.

In engineering, laying the foundation refers to creating a stone or concrete structure that supports a building from underneath. A good foundation is essential for the stability and durability of any construction project, as it bears the weight and load of the entire structure. To lay a good foundation, engineers need to consider factors such as soil type, water level, climate, and design specifications. For example, the Burj Khalifa, the tallest building in the world, has a foundation that consists of 192 piles, each 1.5 meters in diameter and 43 meters long, that are buried 50 meters deep into the ground.

In education, laying the foundation means providing students with the basic knowledge and skills that they need to succeed in their academic and professional careers. A good foundation helps students to develop critical thinking, creativity, communication, and collaboration abilities, as well as a lifelong passion for learning. To lay a good foundation, educators need to design curricula that are relevant, engaging, and challenging for students of different levels and backgrounds. For example, the Laying the Foundation program, developed by the National Math and Science Initiative, offers rigorous and aligned courses in English, math, and science for grades 6–12 that prepare students for college and career readiness.

In science, laying the foundation means conducting research that generates new insights and discoveries that can lead to further innovations and applications. A good foundation expands the frontiers of human knowledge and understanding, and creates opportunities for solving problems and improving lives. To lay a good foundation, scientists need to follow the scientific method, which involves making observations, asking questions, forming hypotheses, testing predictions, analyzing data, and drawing conclusions. For example, Charles Darwin's theory of evolution by natural selection, which he developed after studying the diversity of life on the Galapagos Islands, laid the foundation for the fields of biology, ecology, and genetics.

In business, laying the foundation means establishing the core values and vision that guide the organization's strategy and culture. A good foundation helps the organization to achieve its goals, attract and retain customers and employees, and create a positive impact on society. To lay a good foundation, business leaders need to communicate clearly and consistently the mission, vision, and values of the organization, and align them with the needs and expectations of the stakeholders. For example, Amazon's founder and CEO Jeff Bezos, laid the foundation for the company's success by focusing on customer obsession, innovation, and long-term thinking.

In politics, laying the foundation means creating the policies and institutions that shape the governance and development of a country or region. A good foundation ensures the protection of human rights, the rule of law, the separation of powers, and the participation of the people. To lay a good foundation, politicians need to consult and cooperate with various actors, such as civil society, media, academia, and international partners, and balance the interests and demands of different groups and sectors. For example, the founding fathers of the United States laid the foundation for the country's democracy by drafting and ratifying the Constitution, which defines the principles and structure of the federal government.

Laying the foundation is a vital process that can have significant and lasting effects on various domains and aspects of life. It requires careful planning, execution, and evaluation, as well as the collaboration and contribution of many individuals and organizations. By laying a good foundation, we can create a solid base for building and growing something much larger and better.

Crafting a Vision

Crafting a vision is a vital process for any organization that wants to achieve its long-term goals and aspirations. A vision statement is a clear and concise description of what the organization aims to be in the future, how it will impact the world, and what makes it unique. A well-written vision statement can inspire employees, investors, customers, and other stakeholders to believe in the organization's mission and support its efforts.

However, crafting a vision is not an easy task. It requires creativity, collaboration, and strategic thinking. Here are some steps and tips on how to write a compelling vision statement for your organization.

- Step 1: Define what you do as an output. You should have a high level of clarity on the real activities that your business engages in. Be careful to remain focused on the outcomes and benefits you provide, rather than the features and processes you use. For example, instead of saying "We sell books online," you could say "We empower people to learn and grow through reading".

- Step 2: Define the distinctive contribution that your company makes to the result described above. Next, identify what makes your organization different from others in your industry or sector. What is your competitive advantage, your core value proposition, or your distinctive approach? For example, instead of saying "We empower people to learn and grow through reading," you could say "We empower people to learn and grow through reading personalized recommendations from our community of experts".

- Step 3: Apply some high-level quantification. To make your vision statement more specific and measurable, you can add some numbers or indicators that reflect your desired level of achievement or impact. For example, instead of saying, "We empower people to learn and grow through reading personalized recommendations from our community of experts", you could say, "We empower millions of people to learn and grow through reading personalized recommendations from our community of 10,000 experts".

- Step 4: Add relatable, human, 'real world' aspects. Finally, to make your vision statement more engaging and relatable, you can include some elements that appeal to the emotions, values, or aspirations of your audience. For example, instead of saying, "We empower millions of people to learn and grow through reading personalized recommendations from our community of 10,000 experts", you could say "We empower millions of people to discover new worlds, unlock their potential, and enrich their lives through reading personalized recommendations from our community of 10,000 experts".

Putting it all together, here is an example of a vision statement that follows the above steps:

Our vision is to empower millions of people to discover new worlds, unlock their potential, and enrich their lives through reading personalized recommendations from our community of 10,000 experts.

This vision statement is ambitious, clear, unique, quantifiable, and relatable. It communicates what the organization does, how it does it, why it does it, and who it does it for. It also serves as a guide and a motivator for the organization's future direction and actions.

Setting Goals and Milestones

Setting goals and milestones is a crucial part of any project, whether it is personal or professional. Goals are the desired outcomes or results that one wants to achieve, while milestones are the specific steps or tasks that lead to those outcomes. Setting goals and milestones can help one to:

- Clarify the vision and purpose of the project.

- - Define the project's outcomes and the scope of the work to be done.

- Break down the project into manageable and measurable units.

- Track the progress and performance of the project.

- Celebrate the achievements and learn from the challenges of the project.

To set effective goals and milestones, one should follow the SMART criteria, which stands for Specific, Measurable, Achievable, Relevant, and Time-bound. A SMART goal or milestone is:

- Specific: It clearly states what one wants to accomplish, why it is important, who is involved, where it will take place, and how it will be done.

- Measurable: It has quantifiable indicators or criteria that can be used to assess the success or completion of the goal or milestone.

- Achievable: It is realistic and attainable, considering the available resources, skills, and constraints.

- Relevant: It aligns with the overall vision and purpose of the project, and contributes to the desired outcomes or results.

- Time-bound: It has a clear and reasonable deadline or timeframe for completion.

An example of a SMART goal for a project could be: "To design and launch a new website for our company by June 30, 2024, that will increase our online presence, customer satisfaction, and sales revenue." An example of a SMART milestone for this goal could be: "To create a wireframe and prototype of the new website by March 15, 2024, and get feedback from the stakeholders and potential users."

Setting goals and milestones is not a one-time activity, but a dynamic and iterative process that requires constant monitoring and evaluation. One should regularly review the goals and milestones, and adjust them as needed, based on the feedback, data, and changing circumstances. One should also celebrate the achievements and recognize the efforts of the team members, as well as identify the challenges and lessons learned from the project.

Setting goals and milestones is a key skill for any project manager, leader, or professional. It can help one to plan, execute, and evaluate any project effectively and efficiently, and achieve the desired outcomes or results.

Building a Team

One of the most important skills for any leader is the ability to build and manage a team. A team is a group of people who work together towards a common goal, such as completing a project, solving a problem, or achieving a result. A team can be composed of different members with diverse backgrounds, skills, personalities, and perspectives. Therefore, building a team requires careful planning, communication, coordination, and motivation.

- The first step in building a team is to define the purpose and objectives of the team. The leader should have a clear vision of what the team needs to accomplish, what the standards for success are, and what the time frame and resources are. The leader should also identify the roles and responsibilities of each team member, and assign tasks that align with their interests or areas of expertise. The leader should communicate these expectations to the team members, and ensure that they understand and agree with them.

- The second step in building a team is to foster a positive team culture. The leader should create an environment where team members feel valued, respected, and trusted. The leader should encourage team members to share their ideas, opinions, and feedback, and listen to them attentively. The leader should also promote collaboration, cooperation, and mutual support among team members, and resolve any conflicts or issues that may arise. The leader should also recognize and reward team members for their contributions and achievements, and celebrate team successes.

- The third step in building a team is to monitor and improve team performance. The leader should track the progress and results of the team, and provide regular and constructive feedback to team members. The leader should also solicit feedback from team members on how the team is functioning, and what can be improved. The leader should also facilitate team learning and development, and provide team members with opportunities to enhance their skills, knowledge, and abilities. The leader should also adapt and adjust the team strategy and approach as needed, based on the changing circumstances and challenges.

Building a team is a key skill for effective leadership, as it enables the leader to leverage the collective talents, strengths, and potential of the team members. A well-built team can achieve more than the sum of its parts and deliver high-quality outcomes that meet or exceed the expectations of its stakeholders. A well-built team can also enhance the satisfaction, engagement, and retention of the team members, and foster a sense of belonging and commitment to the team and the organization. Therefore, building a team is a worthwhile and rewarding endeavor for any leader who wants to succeed in today's complex and competitive world.

Defining Success Metrics

Success metrics are quantifiable measurements that business leaders use to track the performance and progress of their strategies, goals, and initiatives. Success metrics are also referred to as key performance indicators (KPIs). Choosing and tracking the right success metrics is essential for making data-driven decisions, aligning work to goals, and assessing strategy efficacy. However, not all success metrics are equally relevant or useful for every product, project, or stakeholder. Therefore, it is important to define success metrics that are specific, measurable, achievable, relevant, and time-bound (SMART).

Specific: Success metrics should be clearly defined and focused on a single aspect of the business. For example, instead of using a vague metric like "customer satisfaction," a more specific metric would be "net promoter score (NPS)," which measures how likely customers are to recommend the product or service to others.

Measurable: Success metrics should be quantifiable and verifiable with data. For example, instead of using a subjective metric like "quality," a more measurable metric would be "defect rate", which measures how many errors or bugs are found in the product or service.

Achievable: Success metrics should be realistic and attainable, based on the available resources, capabilities, and constraints. For example, instead of using an unrealistic metric like "100% market share", a more achievable metric would be "10%

increase in market share", which reflects the current market conditions and competitive landscape.

Relevant: Success metrics should be aligned with the overall vision, mission, and objectives of the business. For example, instead of using an irrelevant metric like "number of likes on social media", a more relevant metric would be "conversion rate", which measures how many visitors become customers or leads.

Time-bound: Success metrics should have a specific timeframe for achieving the desired results. For example, instead of using an indefinite metric like "revenue growth", a more time-bound metric would be "revenue growth in the next quarter", which sets a clear deadline and expectation.

By defining success metrics that are SMART, business leaders can ensure that they are measuring what matters, and that they can communicate their results effectively to their teams and stakeholders. Success metrics can help businesses to evaluate their strengths and weaknesses, identify opportunities and threats, and optimize their strategies and tactics. Success metrics can also help businesses to celebrate their achievements, learn from their failures, and continuously improve their performance.

Chapter 3
Embracing Risk

Risk is often seen as something negative—something to be avoided or minimized. However, risk can also be a source of opportunity, growth, and innovation. Embracing risk means accepting the possibility of failure, but also the potential for success. Embracing risk means being willing to take on challenges, explore new ideas, and learn from mistakes. Embracing risk means being courageous, curious, and creative.

One of the benefits of embracing risk is that it can lead to personal and professional development. By taking risks, we can discover new aspects of ourselves, our abilities, and our interests. We can also develop skills such as problem-solving, decision-making, and resilience. For example, a person who decides to pursue a new career path may face uncertainty and rejection, but also gain valuable experience and knowledge. A person who decides to travel to a foreign country may encounter difficulties and dangers, but also learn about different cultures and perspectives.

Another benefit of embracing risk is that it can foster innovation and progress. By taking risks, we can generate new ideas, products, and solutions. We can also challenge the status quo, question assumptions, and create positive change. For example, a scientist who experiments with a novel hypothesis may fail many times, but also make a breakthrough discovery.

An entrepreneur who launches a new venture may face competition and loss, but also create value and impact.

Of course, embracing risk does not mean being reckless or irresponsible. It means being aware of the risks, weighing the pros and cons, and taking calculated and informed decisions. It also means being prepared for the consequences, both positive and negative, and being ready to adapt and learn. Embracing risk does not guarantee success, but it increases the chances of achieving it.

Embracing risk can be beneficial for both individuals and society as a whole. It can help us grow as people, and contribute to the advancement of humanity. Embracing risk can be scary, but it can also be rewarding. As the famous quote by Mark Twain says, "Twenty years from now, you will be more dissatisfied by what you did not do than what you did." So throw off the bowlines. Sail away from the safe harbor. Catch the trade winds in your sails. Explore. Dream. Discover.

Calculated Risks

What is a calculated risk? A calculated risk is a decision or action that involves weighing the potential benefits and costs of an uncertain outcome. It is not a reckless gamble, but a careful assessment of the possible consequences of a choice. Taking calculated risks is an essential skill for personal and professional growth, as it can help us achieve our goals, discover new possibilities, and overcome our limitations. Taking calculated risks can have positive impacts on our lives, as long as we do it wisely and responsibly.

Taking calculated risks can have many benefits for our personal and professional development.

- Firstly, taking calculated risks can help us learn new skills and acquire new knowledge. For example, if we decide to enroll in a challenging course or pursue a higher degree, we may face some difficulties and obstacles, but we will also gain valuable insights and experience that can enhance our abilities and qualifications.

- Secondly, taking calculated risks can help us expand our opportunities and network. For example, if we decide to apply for a job or a project that is outside our comfort zone, we may encounter some competition and rejection, but we will also expose ourselves to new possibilities and connections that can advance our career and goals.

- Thirdly, taking calculated risks can help us increase our confidence and self-esteem. For example, if we decide to try a new hobby or a sport that is unfamiliar to us, we may feel some anxiety and frustration, but we will also discover our strengths and weaknesses and overcome our fears and doubts.

Taking calculated risks can also have some challenges for our personal and professional well-being.
- Firstly, taking calculated risks can expose us to uncertainty and unpredictability. For example, if we decide to start a new business or invest in a new venture,

we may face some financial and operational risks that can affect our stability and security.

- Secondly, taking calculated risks can trigger fear and stress. For example, if we decide to speak in public or perform in front of an audience, we may experience some nervousness and anxiety that can affect our performance and health.

- Thirdly, taking calculated risks can result in failure and disappointment. For example, if we decide to travel to a new place or explore a new culture, we may encounter some difficulties and challenges that can affect our satisfaction and happiness.

Taking calculated risks effectively requires some planning and preparation. Here are some tips on how to take calculated risks wisely and responsibly.

- Firstly, set realistic and specific goals that are aligned with your values and vision. For example, if you want to improve your health, you can set a goal to exercise regularly or eat more vegetables.

- Secondly, do some research and gather relevant information that can help you make informed decisions. For example, if you want to start a new business, you can do some market analysis or consult some experts.

- Thirdly, seek feedback and support from others who can offer you constructive criticism and encouragement. For example, if you want to speak in public, you can practice with a friend or join a club. Taking calculated risks can be rewarding and fulfilling, but it also requires some courage and commitment.

Taking calculated risks is a vital skill that can help us grow and succeed in various aspects of our lives. Taking calculated risks can bring us many benefits, such as learning new skills, expanding opportunities, and increasing confidence.

However, taking calculated risks can also pose some challenges, such as facing uncertainty, overcoming fear, and dealing with failure. Therefore, we need to take calculated risks wisely and responsibly, by setting realistic goals, doing research, and seeking feedback. Taking calculated risks is not easy, but it is rewarding. As Mark Zuckerberg once said, "The biggest risk is not taking any risk."

Fear of Failure

This is a common emotion that affects many people in different ways. Some people may avoid taking risks or trying new things because they are afraid of failing. Others may procrastinate or give up easily when faced with challenges or difficulties. Fear of failure can also lead to low self-esteem, anxiety, depression, or perfectionism.

However, fear of failure does not have to be a negative or limiting factor in one's life. In fact, failure can be seen as an opportunity to learn, grow, and improve. Failure can teach valuable lessons, such as resilience, persistence, creativity, and humility. Failure can also motivate one to work harder, smarter, and more efficiently. Failure can also help one to discover new possibilities, perspectives, and solutions.

Therefore, instead of fearing failure, one should embrace it as a part of the learning process. One should not let fear of failure stop them from pursuing their goals, dreams, or passions. One should also not let fear of failure define them or their worth. Rather, one should view failure as feedback, not as a final outcome. One should learn from their errors rather than dwelling on them. One should also celebrate their successes, no matter how small or big they are.

To overcome fear of failure, one can adopt some strategies, such as:

- Setting realistic and attainable goals.

- Breaking down large tasks into smaller and more manageable steps.

- Seeking help or guidance from others when needed.

- Focusing on the positive aspects and benefits of the task.

- Rewarding oneself for the efforts and achievements.

- Developing a growth mindset that believes in one's ability to improve and learn.

- Accepting that failure is inevitable and normal in life.

- Reframing failure as a challenge, not as a threat.

Fear of failure is a common and natural emotion that can affect one's performance, behavior, and well-being. However, fear of failure can also be overcome by changing one's attitude and approach towards failure. By seeing failure as an opportunity, not an obstacle, one can overcome their fear of failure and achieve their full potential.

Resilience and Adaptability

These are two interrelated skills that enable people, organizations, and societies to respond effectively to changing and challenging situations. Resilience is the ability to recover from setbacks, cope with stress, and bounce back from adversity. Adaptability is the ability to adjust to new circumstances, learn from feedback, and embrace new opportunities. In the 21st century, these skills are essential for surviving and thriving in a complex and uncertain world.

One of the benefits of resilience and adaptability is that they can help individuals overcome personal challenges that they may face in their lives. For example, resilience can help a person cope with a serious health issue, such as a chronic illness or an injury, by enabling them to accept their situation, seek support, and find meaning in their experience. Adaptability can help a person deal with a financial difficulty, such as a job loss or a debt, by enabling them to explore alternative sources of income, learn new skills, and manage their budget. Similarly, resilience and adaptability can help a person navigate a career transition, such as a promotion or a change of field, by enabling them to embrace the challenge, seek feedback, and adapt to the new environment. These examples show that resilience and adaptability can help individuals overcome personal challenges and achieve their goals.

Another benefit of resilience and adaptability is that they can help organizations cope with external changes that they may encounter in their operations. For example, resilience can help an organization survive a market fluctuation, such as a recession or a crisis, by enabling it to reduce costs, retain customers, and diversify revenue streams. Adaptability can help an organization thrive in a technological innovation, such as a new product or a service, by enabling it to adopt the innovation, train employees, and gain a competitive edge. Likewise, resilience and adaptability can help an organization respond to an environmental crisis, such as a natural disaster or a pandemic, by enabling it to protect employees, maintain continuity, and support recovery. These examples show that resilience and adaptability can help organizations cope with external changes and achieve positive outcomes.

The third benefit of resilience and adaptability is that they can help societies address global issues that they may face in the future. For example, resilience can help a society cope with poverty by enabling it to provide social protection, promote inclusive growth, and reduce inequality. Adaptability can help a society deal with climate change, such as by enabling it to mitigate greenhouse gas emissions, adapt to changing weather patterns, and enhance environmental sustainability. Similarly, resilience and adaptability can help a society tackle other global issues, such as terrorism, migration, or cybercrime, by enabling it to enhance security, foster cooperation, and protect human rights. These examples show that resilience and adaptability can help societies address global issues and achieve positive outcomes.

Resilience and adaptability are two vital skills that can help individuals, organizations, and societies overcome various types of challenges and achieve positive outcomes in the 21st century. Resilience enables people, organizations, and societies to recover from setbacks, cope with stress, and bounce back from adversity. Adaptability enables people, organizations, and societies to adjust to new circumstances, learn from feedback, and embrace new opportunities. Therefore, it is important to develop and enhance these skills through education, training, and practice. By doing so, we can prepare ourselves, our organizations, and our societies for a complex and uncertain future.

Learning from Setbacks

Life is full of challenges and obstacles that sometimes prevent us from achieving our goals or fulfilling our expectations. These are called setbacks, and they can be frustrating, disappointing, and discouraging. However, setbacks are also inevitable and unavoidable, as no one can control everything that happens in life. Therefore, instead of seeing setbacks as failures or dead ends, we should see them as opportunities for learning and growth.

One of the personal setbacks that I have faced in my life was failing an important exam that I had prepared for months. I was devastated and felt like I had wasted my time and effort. However, instead of giving up, I decided to learn from my mistake and improve my study skills. I analyzed where I went wrong, what I could have done better, and how I could avoid similar errors in the future. I also sought feedback from my teacher and peers, and I enrolled in a tutoring program. As a result, I was able to improve my grades, gain more confidence, and develop a growth mindset. This setback taught me that failure is not the end, but a chance to start over with more knowledge and experience.

Another example of a professional setback that I have faced in my career was losing a major client that I had worked with for a long time. I was shocked and saddened by the news, as I had invested a lot of time and energy into building a strong relationship with them. However, instead of dwelling on the loss, I decided to learn from the feedback and improve my performance. I asked the client why they decided to end the contract, what I could have done differently, and how I could meet their expectations better. I also reviewed my work quality, communication skills, and customer service. As a result, I was able to identify my strengths and weaknesses, enhance my skills, and find new opportunities. This setback taught me that change is inevitable, but also a chance to grow and adapt.

Besides learning from specific examples of setbacks, there are also some general tips and strategies that can help us cope with setbacks and turn them into learning experiences. First, we should adopt a positive attitude and view setbacks as challenges, not threats. This can help us reduce stress, increase motivation, and focus on solutions. Second, we should seek support and feedback from others, such as family, friends, mentors, or coaches. They can provide us with emotional, practical, or professional guidance, as well as different perspectives and insights. Third, we should reflect on our goals and actions, and evaluate what we can improve or change. We can use tools such as journals, logs, or plans to track our progress and achievements. Fourth, we should celebrate our successes and appreciate our efforts, no matter how big or small. This can help us boost our self-esteem, confidence, and resilience. These tips and strategies can help us cope with setbacks and turn them into learning experiences.

Setbacks are inevitable and unavoidable in life, but they can also be opportunities for learning and growth. Setbacks can teach us valuable lessons, help us improve ourselves, and lead us to better outcomes. I have provided some examples of personal and professional setbacks that I have faced and how I have learned from them. I have also offered some tips and strategies for coping with setbacks and turning them into learning experiences. I hope this section has inspired you to embrace setbacks as challenges, not threats, and to use them as catalysts for positive change. Remember, every setback is a step forward, if you learn from it.

Chapter 4
Establishing a Brand

Establishing a brand is the process of creating a distinctive identity and image for a business, product, service, or concept in the market. A strong brand can help a business stand out from the competition, attract and retain customers, and communicate its values and purpose.

Here are some steps to follow when establishing a brand:

- Define your brand's purpose and position.

- What is the reason your brand exists?

- What problem does it solve or what value does it provide for your target audience?

- How is it different from other brands in the same category?

- What is the unique selling proposition or benefit that your brand offers?

- Develop a personality and brand voice.

- How do you want your brand to sound and feel?

- What tone, style, and language do you use to communicate with your audience?

- What are the traits and characteristics that define your brand's character?

Your brand's personality and voice should reflect your brand's purpose and position and appeal to your ideal customer.

Create your brand story.

What is the narrative or story behind your brand? How did it start, what challenges did it overcome, what milestones did it achieve, and what goals does it have for the future? Your brand story should be authentic, engaging, and memorable, and it should convey your brand's mission, vision, and values.

Pick a brand name. What is the name of your brand? It should be catchy, easy to remember, and relevant to your brand's purpose and position. It should also be available as a domain name, trademark, and social media handle. You can use tools like a business name generator or domain name search to help you come up with ideas.

Write a slogan. What is the tagline or catchphrase that summarizes your brand's essence or promise? It should be short, catchy, and memorable, and reinforce your brand's name, position, and personality. You can use tools like slogan generators or rhyme zones to help you craft a slogan.

Design your brand's look and logo. What are the visual elements that represent your brand? You should choose a color palette, typography, imagery, and iconography that suit your brand's personality and voice, and create a consistent and recognizable brand identity. Your logo should be simple, distinctive, and scalable, and reflect your brand name, slogan, and story. You can use tools like a logo maker or a color wheel to help you design a logo.

Integrate your brand into your business. How do you apply your brand identity and voice to every aspect of your business? You should create a brand style guide that outlines the rules and standards for using your brand elements across different channels and platforms, such as your website, social media, email, packaging, signage, etc. You should also train your employees and partners on how to represent your brand consistently and effectively.

Promote your brand. How do you raise awareness and recognition of your brand among your target audience and the market? You should use various marketing strategies and tactics to showcase your brand's value proposition, story, and personality, and reach your potential and existing customers. You can use tools like [social media marketing] or [email marketing] to help you promote your brand.

Monitor and improve your brand. How do you measure and evaluate the performance and perception of your brand? You should use various metrics and feedback tools to track and analyze how your brand is doing in terms of awareness, reputation, loyalty, and satisfaction. You should also seek to improve your brand by adapting to changing customer needs, preferences, and expectations, and by innovating and evolving your brand offerings and experiences.

These are some of the steps to follow when establishing a brand. By following these steps, you can create a brand that is distinctive, trustworthy, memorable, and likable to your target audience, which can help you achieve your business goals and objectives.

Brand Identity and Values

Identity and Values are two interrelated concepts that shape how a business is perceived and experienced by its customers, employees, and other stakeholders. Brand identity is the visual and emotional representation of a brand, while brand values are the foundational beliefs that a brand stands for. In this essay, I will explain why brand identity and values are important for any business, and how they can be developed and communicated effectively.

Brand identity and values are important for several reasons.
- Firstly they help a business differentiate itself from the competition and create a unique position in the market. A strong brand identity and values can convey a clear and consistent message about what the business offers, how it delivers value, and why it matters. For example, Apple's brand identity and values are based on innovation, design, and simplicity, which distinguish it from other technology companies and attract loyal customers.

- Secondly, brand identity and values help a business build trust and loyalty with its customers and employees. A strong brand identity and values can create an emotional connection and a sense of belonging among the people who interact with the brand. Customers and employees who share the same values as the brand are more likely to be satisfied, engaged, and loyal. For example, Patagonia's brand identity and values are based on environmental and social responsibility, which resonate with its customers and employees who care about these issues.

- Thirdly, brand identity and values help a business achieve its purpose and vision. A strong brand identity and values can provide a clear direction and motivation for the business and its stakeholders. They can also inspire innovation and creativity, as well as drive performance and growth. For example, Tesla's brand identity and values are based on accelerating the transition to sustainable energy, which guides its product development and business strategy.

To develop and communicate a strong brand identity and values, a business needs to follow a few steps. First, it needs to define its purpose, vision, mission, and values, which are the core elements of its brand strategy. These should reflect what the business stands for, what it aims to achieve, and how it plans to do it. Second, it needs to design its brand identity, which includes elements such as the logo, color palette, typography, imagery, and messaging. These should reflect the brand's personality, tone, and style, and be consistent across all touchpoints. Third, it needs to deliver its brand values, which means living up to its promises and expectations. This involves aligning the business's actions, decisions, and culture with its values, and demonstrating them through its products, services, and interactions.

Brand identity and values are essential for any business that wants to succeed in a competitive and dynamic market. They help a business differentiate itself, build trust and loyalty, and achieve its goals. To create a strong brand identity and values, a business needs to define, design, and deliver them effectively.

Brand Strategies

Brand Strategies are the plans and actions that a business takes to create and maintain a distinctive and favorable image in the minds of its customers and potential customers. A brand strategy guides every aspect of a business's branding, from its name, logo, and colors, to its voice, storytelling, and values. A brand strategy also defines how a business differentiates itself from its competitors and positions itself in the market.

Why are brand strategies important?

Brand strategies are important for several reasons. First, they help a business build a strong and consistent brand identity that reflects its purpose, vision, and personality. A clear and coherent brand identity can help a business attract and retain loyal customers, as well as inspire trust and confidence in its products and services. Second, they help a business communicate its value proposition and unique selling points to its target audience. A compelling and relevant value proposition can help a business stand out from the crowd and persuade customers to choose its brand over others. Third, they help a business align its internal and external stakeholders around a common goal and direction. A shared and well-defined brand strategy can help a business foster a culture of collaboration, innovation, and excellence among its employees, partners, and suppliers.

How to create a brand strategy?

Creating a brand strategy involves several steps and elements. Here is a simplified overview of the process:

- Define your brand's purpose. This is the reason why your business exists and what it aims to achieve. Your brand purpose should be aligned with your business mission, vision, and values, and it should answer the question: How does your business make a positive impact on the world?
- Define your target audience. This is the group of people who are most likely to benefit from your products and services, and who you want to reach and engage with your brand. Your target audience should be based on market research and customer insights, and should answer the question: Who are your ideal customers and what are their needs, wants, and preferences?
- Define your brand positioning. This is the way you want your brand to be perceived and remembered by your target audience. Your brand positioning should be based on your competitive analysis and value proposition, and it should answer the question: How does your brand differ from and excel over your competitors?
- Define your brand identity. This is the visual and verbal expression of your brand, including your name, logo, colors, fonts, tone of voice, tagline, and slogan. Your

brand identity should be based on your brand personality and style, and it should answer the question: How does your brand look and sound like?
- Define your brand story. This is the narrative that connects your brand with your target audience on an emotional level. Your brand story should be based on your brand history and values, and should answer the question: What is the story behind your brand and why should your audience care?
- Define your brand touchpoints. These are the points of contact and interaction between your brand and your target audience, such as your website, social media, packaging, advertising, and customer service. Your brand touchpoints should be based on your brand strategy and objectives, and should answer the question: How does your brand deliver its value and message to your audience?

A brand strategy is not a one-time project, but a continuous process that requires constant evaluation and improvement. A successful brand strategy can help a business create a powerful and memorable brand that resonates with its customers and stands out in the market.

Positioning in the Market

This is the process of creating a distinctive image and identity for a product or service in the minds of the target customers. It involves highlighting the unique attributes and benefits of the product or service that differentiate it from the competitors and appeal to the customers' needs and preferences. Positioning in the market is a key to success for any business, as it helps to establish a competitive advantage, attract and retain customers, and enhance the brand value and reputation.

There are different types of positioning strategies that a business can adopt, depending on the product, market, and customer segments. Some of the common types of positioning strategies are:

- **Pricing:** This strategy involves positioning the product or service as either low-cost or premium, depending on the target market and the value proposition. For example, Walmart positions itself as a low-cost retailer that offers everyday low prices, while Apple positions itself as a premium brand that offers high-quality and innovative products.

- **Quality:** This strategy involves positioning the product or service as superior or inferior in quality compared to the competitors. For example, Toyota positions itself as a reliable and durable car manufacturer that offers quality vehicles, while Kia positions itself as a budget-friendly and practical car maker that offers value for money.

- **Differentiation:** This strategy involves positioning the product or service as unique or different from the competitors in terms of features, benefits, design, or performance. For example, Netflix positions itself as a leading online streaming service that offers original and exclusive content, while Disney+ positions itself as a family-friendly streaming service that offers classic and nostalgic content.

- **Convenience:** This strategy involves positioning the product or service as easy or difficult to access, use, or maintain compared to its competitors. For example, Amazon positions itself as a convenient online marketplace that offers fast and free delivery, while Ikea positions itself as a do-it-yourself furniture store that offers affordable and customizable products.

- **Customer service:** This strategy involves positioning the product or service as friendly or unfriendly, responsive or unresponsive, or helpful or unhelpful compared to the competitors. For example, Zappos positions itself as a customer-centric online shoe store that offers free shipping and returns, while Comcast positions itself as a notorious cable provider that offers poor customer service.

To create an effective positioning strategy, a business needs to follow these steps:

- **Find the current position:** This step involves analyzing the current image and perception of the product or service in the market and among the customers. It also involves identifying the strengths and weaknesses of the product or service, as well as the opportunities and threats in the market.

- **Analyze the competitors:** This step involves researching and evaluating the competitors' products, services, prices, quality, features, benefits, and customer service. It also involves identifying the gaps and niches in the market that the competitors are not addressing or serving well.

- **Develop a unique position:** This step involves defining the unique value proposition and the core message that the product or service wants to communicate to the customers. It also involves choosing the type of positioning strategy that best suits the product, market, and customer segments.

- **Create a positioning statement:** This step involves crafting a concise and clear statement that summarizes the product or service, the target market, the point of difference, and the reason to buy. For example, the positioning statement of Volvo is: "For upscale American families, Volvo is the family automobile that offers maximum safety."

- **Create a tagline:** This step involves creating a catchy and memorable slogan that reinforces the positioning statement and the brand identity. For example, the tagline of L'Oréal is: "Because you're worth it."

- Test the positioning strategy: This step involves testing and validating the positioning strategy with the target customers and the market. It also involves collecting feedback and measuring the effectiveness and impact of the positioning strategy on customer satisfaction, loyalty, and retention.

Positioning in the market is a vital and ongoing process that requires constant research, analysis, and evaluation. A successful positioning strategy can help a business to stand out from the crowd, create a loyal customer base, and achieve a sustainable competitive edge.

Customer Engagement

Customer engagement is the process of building and maintaining relationships with customers at every touch point. It involves understanding customer needs, preferences, and pain points, and delivering value at every interaction. Customer engagement is crucial for businesses seeking to create loyal and satisfied customers, increase retention and revenue, and enhance brand reputation.

One of the first steps to engaging customers is to understand the difference between customer engagement, customer experience, and customer relationship management (CRM). Customer experience refers to the overall perception and feeling that customers have when interacting with a brand or product. It encompasses all aspects of the customer journey, from awareness to loyalty. CRM is the process of managing and optimizing the interactions and relationships with existing and potential customers. It involves using data and technology to segment, target, and communicate with customers. Customer engagement is a subset of customer experience and CRM that focuses on creating meaningful and valuable interactions with customers at every touch point. It involves personalizing customer experiences, providing consistent and relevant messages, soliciting and acting on feedback, and building trust and loyalty. Some examples of customer engagement strategies are creating a brand voice, offering personalized service, implementing a chatbot, and using social media contests. These strategies can help businesses improve customer experience and CRM by increasing customer satisfaction, retention, and advocacy.

Customer engagement faces new challenges and opportunities in the digital age. Technology, data, and social media have transformed the way customers interact with brands and products. Customers now have more choices, information, and power than ever before. They expect fast, convenient, and personalized experiences across multiple channels and devices. They also seek authentic and meaningful connections with brands that share their values and interests. To meet these expectations, businesses need to leverage technology, data, and social media to enhance customer engagement. Technology can help businesses create seamless and integrated experiences across the customer journey, from awareness to loyalty. Data can help businesses understand customer behavior, preferences, and needs, and provide relevant and timely offers and solutions. Social media can help businesses communicate with customers, build communities, and generate word-of-mouth. Some examples of how businesses can use technology, data, and social media to improve customer engagement are creating mobile apps, using chatbots and artificial intelligence, implementing loyalty programs, and creating user-generated content campaigns. These methods can help businesses increase customer satisfaction, retention, and advocacy in the digital age.

Another important aspect of customer engagement is to evaluate the best practices and metrics for measuring it. Metrics are indicators that help businesses track and assess the performance and effectiveness of their customer engagement strategies.

There are two types of metrics: quantitative and qualitative.

- Quantitative metrics are numerical and objective, such as the number of visits, conversions, or referrals.

- Qualitative metrics are both descriptive and subjective, such as the level of satisfaction, loyalty, or advocacy. Both types of metrics have advantages and disadvantages.

Quantitative metrics are easy to collect and analyze, but they may not capture the full picture of customer engagement.

Qualitative metrics are more insightful and meaningful, but they may be difficult to obtain and interpret. Some examples of customer engagement metrics are Net Promoter Score (NPS), Customer Satisfaction Score (CSAT), Customer Lifetime Value (CLV), Customer Health Score, and Daily Active Users (DAU). These metrics can help businesses monitor and optimize customer engagement by identifying the strengths and weaknesses of their customer engagement strategies, and by providing feedback and insights for improvement.

Customer engagement is not only a marketing strategy, but also a competitive advantage and a source of innovation for businesses in the digital age. Customer engagement involves creating meaningful and valuable interactions with customers at every touch point, using technology, data, and social media to enhance the customer experience and CRM, and measuring customer engagement using both quantitative and qualitative metrics. By engaging customers effectively, businesses can increase customer satisfaction, retention, and advocacy, ultimately driving business growth. However, customer engagement also poses new challenges and opportunities for businesses, such as understanding customer preferences, adapting to changing customer behavior, and managing customer feedback. Therefore, future research and practice on customer engagement should explore how to overcome these challenges and leverage these opportunities, as well as how to design and implement customer engagement marketing initiatives that are aligned with the firm's goals and values.

EXPAND

Chapter 5

Scaling Operations

Scaling operations is the process of increasing or decreasing the capacity and efficiency of a business to meet the changing demand for its products or services. It is a crucial aspect of business growth and competitiveness, as it enables a business to adapt to the market conditions and customer expectations. However, scaling operations is not a simple or straightforward task. It requires careful planning, execution, and evaluation of various factors, such as the following:

- **The current state of the business operations:** Before scaling up or down, a business needs to assess its current operational performance, strengths, weaknesses, opportunities, and threats. This can help identify the areas that need improvement, the resources that are available or needed, and the potential risks or challenges that may arise during the scaling process.

- **The goals and objectives of the scaling process:** A business needs to have a clear vision and purpose for scaling its operations. It should define the specific outcomes and benefits that it expects to achieve, such as increasing revenue, market share, customer satisfaction, or innovation. It should also set realistic and measurable targets and indicators to track and evaluate the progress and results of the scaling process.

- **The strategies and methods for scaling operations:** A business needs to choose the most suitable and effective ways to scale its operations, depending on its goals, resources, and capabilities. Some of the common strategies and methods for scaling operations include:

- **Automating processes:** This involves using technology, such as software, hardware, or artificial intelligence, to perform tasks that were previously done manually or with human intervention. This can help increase the speed, accuracy, consistency, and quality of the operations, as well as reduce the costs, errors, and risks involved.

- **Outsourcing processes:** This involves delegating or transferring some or all of the operations to external parties, such as vendors, contractors, or consultants. This can help access specialized skills, expertise, or equipment that the business may not have internally, as well as reduce the workload, complexity, and overhead of the operations.

- **Standardizing processes:** This involves creating and implementing uniform rules, procedures, or guidelines for the operations, such as best practices, policies, or quality standards. This can help ensure the consistency, reliability, and compliance of the operations, as well as facilitate the coordination, communication, and collaboration among the operational teams or units.

- **Optimizing processes:** This involves analyzing and improving the efficiency and effectiveness of the operations, such as by eliminating waste, reducing variation, or enhancing value. This can help increase the productivity, profitability, and customer satisfaction of the operations, as well as enable the business to respond faster and better to the changing demand or feedback.

The challenges and risks of scaling operations: A business needs to anticipate and mitigate the potential difficulties or drawbacks that may arise during or after the scaling process, such as:

- **Loss of control or quality:** Scaling operations may result in a loss of direct oversight or involvement in the operations, which may affect the quality, accuracy, or timeliness of the output or service. To prevent or minimize this, a business needs to establish and maintain clear and effective communication, monitoring, and feedback mechanisms with the internal or external parties involved in the operations.

- **Resistance or disruption:** Scaling operations may encounter resistance or disruption from the internal or external stakeholders, such as employees, customers, or competitors. This may affect the morale, motivation, or loyalty of the stakeholders, or create conflicts or complaints. To prevent or minimize this, a business needs to communicate and engage with the stakeholders and address their concerns or expectations, before, during, and after the scaling process.

- **Complexity or uncertainty:** Scaling operations may increase the complexity or uncertainty of the operations, such as by introducing new processes, systems, or technologies, or changing the existing ones. This may affect the stability, reliability, or security of the operations, or create errors or failures. To prevent or minimize this, a business needs to test and validate the feasibility, functionality, and compatibility of the scaling solutions, and provide adequate training, support, or backup for the operational staff or users.

Scaling operations is a vital and challenging process for any business that wants to grow and succeed in a competitive and dynamic market. It requires careful and strategic planning, execution, and evaluation, as well as constant monitoring and improvement, to ensure that the scaling process is aligned with the business goals, objectives, and values, and delivers the desired outcomes and benefits for the business and its stakeholders.

Operational Efficiency

Operational efficiency is the ability of a business to produce optimal output with minimal input or waste. It is a measure of how well a company utilizes its resources to achieve its goals and objectives. Operational efficiency can be expressed as the ratio of operating expenses to total revenue, where a lower ratio indicates higher efficiency.

Operational efficiency is important for businesses because it can enhance their profitability, competitiveness, and customer satisfaction. By reducing costs and increasing productivity, operational efficiency can improve the bottom line and create a competitive advantage. Additionally, operational efficiency can improve the quality and reliability of products and services, leading to higher customer loyalty and retention.

There are several steps that businesses can take to improve their operational efficiency, such as:

- **Streamlining processes:** Businesses can identify and eliminate unnecessary or redundant steps in their workflows, such as duplication, rework, or delays. This can save time, money, and resources, and increase the speed and accuracy of output.

- **Investing in technology:** Businesses can leverage technology to automate, optimize, and integrate their processes, such as using software, cloud computing, artificial intelligence, or robotics. This can reduce human errors, enhance collaboration, and enable scalability and innovation.

- **Training employees:** Businesses can provide regular training and development opportunities for their employees, such as coaching, mentoring, or online courses. This can improve their skills, knowledge, and performance, and increase their motivation and engagement.

- **Measuring and monitoring:** Businesses can establish and track key performance indicators (KPIs) and metrics for their processes, such as quality, efficiency, or customer satisfaction. This can help them evaluate their performance, identify gaps and opportunities, and implement corrective and preventive actions.

- **Benchmarking and learning:** Businesses can compare their performance and practices with their competitors or industry standards, such as using SWOT analysis, Porter's five forces, or best practices. This can help them learn from others, gain insights, and adopt strategies to improve their operational efficiency.

Operational efficiency is a vital factor for business success, as it can increase profitability, competitiveness, and customer satisfaction. Businesses can improve their operational efficiency by streamlining processes, investing in technology, training employees, measuring and monitoring, and benchmarking and learning. By doing so, they can optimize their resource utilization and achieve their desired outcomes.

Managing Growth

Growth is a desirable goal for any business, as it implies increased revenue, market share, and competitive advantage. However, growth also brings many challenges, such as maintaining quality, satisfying customers, managing resources, and adapting to change. Therefore, businesses need to adopt effective strategies to manage growth and overcome the potential pitfalls.

- One of the main challenges of growth is maintaining quality and consistency across the business. As the business expands, it may face difficulties in ensuring that all its products, services, processes, and standards meet the expectations of its customers and stakeholders. Quality issues can damage the reputation and profitability of the business, as well as expose it to legal and regulatory risks. To address this challenge, businesses need to implement quality management systems, such as ISO 9001, that define the policies, procedures, and responsibilities for achieving quality objectives. Businesses also need to monitor and measure their performance, collect feedback, and implement continuous improvement initiatives.

- Another challenge of growth is satisfying the diverse and changing needs of customers. As the business grows, it may encounter new segments, markets, and preferences that require different approaches and solutions. Customers may also have higher expectations and demands, as they compare the business with its competitors and alternatives. To address this challenge, businesses need to adopt a customer-centric mindset, that focuses on understanding and fulfilling the needs and wants of customers. Businesses also need to invest in market research, customer relationship management, and innovation, to create value and loyalty for their customers.

- The third challenge of growth is managing the resources and capabilities of the business. As the business grows, it may need more human, financial, and physical resources to support its operations and activities. However, these resources may not be readily available or sufficient, especially in times of uncertainty or volatility. Moreover, the business may face difficulties in coordinating and integrating its resources, as it becomes more complex and diverse. To address this challenge, businesses need to plan and allocate their resources strategically, based on their goals and priorities. Businesses also need to optimize their processes, systems, and structures, to improve efficiency and effectiveness.

- The fourth challenge of growth is adapting to the external and internal changes that affect the business. As the business grows, it may face new opportunities and threats in the environment, such as technological, social, economic, and political factors. The business may also experience changes in its culture, values, and vision, as it evolves and matures. To address this challenge, businesses need to be agile and flexible, able to respond quickly and creatively to the changing conditions. Businesses also need to foster a culture of learning and innovation, that encourages experimentation, collaboration, and feedback.

Growth is a double-edged sword for businesses, as it brings both benefits and challenges. To manage growth successfully, businesses need to adopt strategies that address the quality, customer, resource, and change challenges that they face. By doing so, businesses can leverage their growth potential and achieve sustainable and competitive advantages.

Technology Integration

Technology integration is the well-organized use of digital devices and cloud computing as instruments for problem-solving, deeper learning, and understanding. It involves the incorporation of technology resources and tools into various aspects of an organization's or individual's activities to enhance and streamline processes, improve productivity, and achieve specific goals. Technology integration can also support classroom instruction by creating opportunities for students to complete assignments on the computer rather than with normal pencil and paper.

Technology integration is not simply using technology for its own sake, but rather using it as a means to an end. Technology should serve the curriculum and the learning objectives, not the other way around. Technology integration requires a shift in mindset from treating technology as a separate subject to seeing it as a tool that can be applied across disciplines and contexts. Technology integration also requires a pedagogical change from teacher-centered to student-centered approaches, where students are given more autonomy, choice, and responsibility for their own learning.

Some of the benefits of technology integration are:
- It can increase student engagement, motivation, and interest in learning.

- It can foster collaboration, communication, and creativity among students and teachers.

- It can provide access to a variety of information sources, perspectives, and experts.

- It can enhance differentiation, personalization, and the scaffolding of learning.

- It can facilitate feedback, assessment, and reflection on learning.

- It can develop digital literacy, critical thinking, and problem-solving skills.

Some of the challenges of technology integration are:

- It can require a significant investment in infrastructure, equipment, maintenance, and training.

- It can pose ethical, legal, and safety issues related to privacy, security, and cyberbullying.

- It can create a digital divide and inequity among students and teachers with different levels of access and proficiency.

- It can cause distraction, overload, and dependence on technology.

- It can create resistance, anxiety, and frustration among students and teachers who are not comfortable or familiar with technology.

To overcome these challenges, technology integration requires a strategic and systematic approach that involves planning, implementation, evaluation, and improvement. Technology integration should be aligned with the vision, mission, and goals of the organization or individual and should be supported by adequate resources, policies, and professional development. Technology integration should also be based on sound pedagogical principles, research evidence, and best practices. Technology integration should be flexible, adaptable, and responsive to the needs, interests, and abilities of the students and teachers.

Technology integration is not a one-time event, but a continuous process of learning and innovation. Technology integration is not a destination, but a journey of exploration and discovery. Technology integration is not a challenge, but an opportunity to transform education and society.

Supply Chain Optimization

Supply chain optimization is the process of improving the efficiency, cost-effectiveness, and sustainability of a supply chain. A supply chain is a network of entities that are involved in the production, distribution, and consumption of goods and services. Supply chain optimization aims to align the supply chain with the customer demand, reduce waste and risk, increase profitability and competitiveness, and enhance customer satisfaction.

There are three main phases of supply chain optimization: design, planning, and execution. In the design phase, the supply chain is configured to meet the strategic objectives of the organization, such as market share, revenue, and customer service. The design phase involves decisions such as where to locate the facilities, how to source the materials and components, how to transport the products, and how to manage the inventory. The design phase can use tools such as network optimization, simulation, and scenario analysis to evaluate different alternatives and trade-offs.

In the planning phase, the supply chain is coordinated to match the demand and supply in the short and medium term. The planning phase involves decisions such as how much to produce, how much to order, how to allocate the resources, and how to respond to changes in the market conditions. The planning phase can use tools such as forecasting, inventory optimization, production planning, and replenishment planning to balance the supply and demand, minimize the costs, and maximize the service levels.

In the execution phase, the supply chain is monitored and controlled to ensure the smooth and timely flow of goods and information. The execution phase involves decisions such as how to track the shipments, how to handle the exceptions, how to communicate with the partners, and how to measure the performance. The execution phase can use tools such as transportation management, warehouse management, order management, and supply chain visibility to optimize the operations, improve the quality, and increase agility.

Supply chain optimization is not a one-time activity, but a continuous process that requires constant adaptation and improvement. Supply chain optimization can leverage technologies such as artificial intelligence, blockchain, and the internet to enhance the capabilities and outcomes of the supply chain. For example, artificial intelligence can provide insights and recommendations based on data analysis and machine learning, blockchain can provide transparency and security based on distributed ledgers and smart contracts; and the internet can provide connectivity and automation based on sensors and devices.

Supply chain optimization can provide various benefits for the organization, such as lower costs, higher revenues, better customer service, and greater sustainability. Supply chain optimization can also provide benefits for the society and the environment, such as reduced emissions, less waste, and more social responsibility. Supply chain optimization is a key factor for achieving competitive advantage and creating value in the global and dynamic market.

Chapter 6

Expanding Horizons

One of the most rewarding aspects of life is learning new things. Whether it is a new skill, a new language, a new hobby, or a new perspective, learning something new can enrich our lives in many ways. In this essay, I will discuss some of the benefits of learning new things, such as enhancing our cognitive abilities, improving our well-being, and broadening our worldview.

Firstly, learning new things can enhance our cognitive abilities, such as memory, creativity, and problem-solving. According to research, learning new and challenging things can stimulate the growth of new brain cells and connections, which can improve our mental performance and prevent cognitive decline. For example, learning a musical instrument can improve our auditory and motor skills, learning a foreign language can improve our verbal and cultural skills, and learning a game like chess can improve our logical and strategic skills. By learning new things, we can keep our brains active and healthy, and increase our intellectual potential.

Secondly, learning new things can improve our well-being, such as happiness, confidence, and resilience. According to research, learning new things can increase our self-esteem, self-efficacy, and self-regulation, which can boost our mood and motivation. For example, learning a new sport can increase our physical fitness, learning a new art form can increase our self-expression, and learning a new topic can increase our curiosity. By learning new things, we can discover new passions, challenge ourselves, and achieve our goals.

Thirdly, learning new things can broaden our worldview, such as empathy, diversity, and tolerance. According to research, learning new things can expose us to different cultures, perspectives, and experiences, which can enhance our social and emotional skills. For example, learning about history can increase our awareness of the past, learning about science can increase our understanding of the present, and learning about philosophy can increase our vision of the future. By learning new things, we can appreciate the complexity and beauty of the world, and connect with others who share our interests.

Learning new things can benefit us in many ways, such as enhancing our cognitive abilities, improving our well-being, and broadening our worldview. Learning new things can also make our lives more enjoyable, meaningful, and fulfilling. Therefore, I believe that we should always seek to learn new things and expand our horizons.

Market Expansion Strategies

Market expansion strategies are growth strategies that aim to make a product or service available in new markets when existing ones get saturated. It may take several forms, including adding a product or service to the portfolio, introducing existing goods or services globally or changing current products or services. A market expansion strategy can help a business to acquire new assets and resources, diversify risk, and gain a competitive advantage. However, market expansion also involves challenges and risks, such as cultural differences, legal barriers, and increased competition. Therefore, a market expansion strategy should be carefully planned and executed, following these steps:

- **Define goals and objectives:** A clear vision of what the business wants to achieve and how to measure success is essential for any market expansion strategy. The goals

and objectives should be specific, measurable, achievable, relevant, and time-bound (SMART).
- **Build a strong team:** A market expansion strategy requires a team of experts and professionals who can handle different aspects of the project, such as market research, product development, marketing, sales, finance, and legal. The team should have a clear division of roles and responsibilities, as well as effective communication and collaboration skills.
- **Conduct market research:** A thorough analysis of the potential markets is crucial for identifying the best opportunities and challenges for market expansion. The market research should include both primary and secondary data, such as customer needs and preferences, market size and growth, competitive landscape, regulatory environment, and cultural factors.
- **Create a financial plan:** A market expansion strategy should have a realistic and detailed budget that covers all the costs and revenues associated with the project. The financial plan should also include a break-even analysis, a cash flow projection, and a risk assessment.
- **Learn from competitors:** A market expansion strategy should take into account the strengths and weaknesses of the existing and potential competitors in the new markets. The business should learn from the best practices and avoid the mistakes of the competitors, as well as differentiate itself from them by offering a unique value proposition.
- **Integrate localization from the start:** A market expansion strategy should consider the local needs and expectations of the customers in the new markets. The business should adapt its products or services, as well as

its marketing and sales strategies, to the local language, culture, and preferences. Localization can help the business to build trust and loyalty among its customers, as well as comply with the local laws and regulations.

A market expansion strategy is a powerful way to grow a business and reach new customers. However, it also requires careful planning and execution, as well as constant monitoring and evaluation. A successful market expansion strategy should be based on a clear vision, a strong team, a thorough market research, a realistic financial plan, a competitive analysis, and a localization strategy. By following these steps, a business can create a market expansion strategy that drives global growth.

International Growth

International growth is the process of expanding a business or organization beyond its domestic market and into new regions or countries. International growth can offer many benefits, such as access to larger and more diverse customer bases, increased revenue and profitability, enhanced innovation and competitiveness, and reduced dependence on a single market. However, international growth also poses many challenges, such as cultural and legal differences, political and economic risks, logistical and operational complexities, and increased competition and costs.

To achieve successful international growth, a business or organization needs to adopt a strategic approach that considers the following factors:

- **Market selection:** The business or organization should identify and evaluate the potential markets that offer the most attractive opportunities for its products or services, based on factors such as market size, growth, demand, competition, and barriers to entry.

- **Market entry mode:** The business or organization should choose the most appropriate way to enter the selected markets through exporting, licensing, franchising, joint ventures, strategic alliances, or foreign direct investment. The choice of entry mode depends on factors such as the level of control, risk, commitment, and resources required by the business or organization.

- **Market adaptation:** The business or organization should adapt its products or services, marketing mix, and organizational structure to suit the preferences, needs, and expectations of the local customers, partners, and stakeholders. The degree of adaptation depends on factors such as the level of similarity or difference between the home and host markets, the degree of standardization or customization required by the products or services, and the degree of integration or differentiation desired by the business or organization.

- **Market performance:** The business or organization should monitor and evaluate its performance in international markets using metrics such as sales, market share, profitability, customer satisfaction, and brand awareness. The business or organization should also identify and address any issues or problems that may arise, such as customer complaints, quality issues, legal disputes, or regulatory changes.

International growth can be a rewarding strategy for a business or organization that seeks to expand its horizons and reach new customers. However, international growth also requires careful planning, execution, and evaluation, as well as a willingness to adapt and learn from the new markets. By following a strategic approach that considers the market selection, entry mode, adaptation, and performance factors, a business or organization can increase its chances of achieving successful international growth.

Strategic Partnership

A strategic partnership is a collaborative alliance between two or more businesses or organizations that share common interests and goals. The purpose of a strategic partnership is to leverage each other's strengths, resources, and expertise to create value for both parties and their customers. Strategic partnerships can take various forms, such as marketing, product development, distribution, research and development, etc. Some examples of successful strategic partnerships are Apple and Nike, Starbucks and Spotify, and Ford and Rivian. These partnerships have enabled the companies to offer innovative products and services, reach new markets, and gain a competitive advantage. However, strategic partnerships are not without challenges and risks. They require careful planning, clear communication, and mutual trust to ensure alignment and compatibility. This essay will discuss the types, benefits, challenges, and best practices of strategic partnerships.

There are different types of strategic partnerships, depending on the nature and scope of the collaboration. Marketing partnerships involve promoting each other's products or services to increase brand awareness and customer loyalty. For instance, Starbucks and Spotify have partnered to create a personalized music experience for Starbucks customers, who can access Spotify playlists and earn rewards through the Starbucks app. Product development partnerships involve creating or enhancing products or services that complement each other's offerings. For example, Apple and Nike have partnered to create the Nike+ iPod, a device that tracks and syncs the user's workout data using their iPod and Nike shoes. Distribution partnerships involve sharing or expanding each other's channels or platforms to reach new customers or markets. For example, Ford and Rivian have partnered to use Rivian's electric vehicle platform to produce Ford's first all-electric pickup truck. Research and development partnerships involve sharing or co-investing in research and innovation projects to solve common problems or explore new opportunities. For example, Google and NASA have partnered to use Google's quantum computer to advance NASA's research in artificial intelligence and machine learning. These types of strategic partnerships can offer various advantages, such as increasing revenue, reducing costs, enhancing quality, and accelerating innovation. However, they also pose some disadvantages, such as losing control, sharing confidential information, facing legal issues, and encountering cultural differences.

The formation of strategic partnerships is influenced by various factors, such as market conditions, customer needs, industry trends, etc. Businesses may seek strategic partnerships to respond to changing customer preferences, enter new markets, access new technologies, or overcome barriers to entry. Strategic partnerships can provide several benefits, such as increasing customer satisfaction, expanding market share, improving profitability, and gaining a competitive edge. However, strategic partnerships also entail some challenges, such as aligning objectives, roles, and expectations, establishing effective communication channels, resolving conflicts, and measuring performance and outcomes. Therefore, businesses need to carefully assess the potential benefits and risks of entering into a strategic partnership and choose the right partner that shares their vision, values, and goals.

The success of a strategic partnership depends largely on how well it is created and managed. There are some best practices that can help businesses create and maintain a successful strategic partnership, such as setting clear objectives, roles, and expectations, establishing effective communication channels, resolving conflicts, and evaluating performance and outcomes. Setting clear objectives, roles, and expectations helps to define the scope, purpose, and deliverables of the partnership and avoid misunderstandings and disagreements. Establishing effective communication channels helps to facilitate information sharing, feedback, and coordination and build trust and rapport. Resolving conflicts helps to address issues and concerns and maintain a positive and constructive relationship. Evaluating performance and outcomes helps to monitor progress, identify problems, and make adjustments and improvements.

Strategic partnerships are a powerful way for businesses to achieve their goals and create value for their customers. However, strategic partnerships are not easy to form and manage. They require careful planning, clear communication, and mutual trust to ensure alignment and compatibility. Strategic partnerships can offer various opportunities and advantages, but they also pose some risks and difficulties. Therefore, businesses need to carefully assess the potential benefits and risks of entering into a strategic partnership and choose the right partner that shares their vision, values, and goals. Strategic partnerships can be a key to business success if they are well-designed and well-executed.

Diversification

Diversification is a risk management approach that combines a variety of investments within a portfolio. A diversified portfolio consists of different kinds of assets and investment vehicles designed to restrict exposure to any particular asset or risk. The basis for this method is that a portfolio made up of several types of assets would, on average, provide greater long-term returns while lowering the risk of any given holding or security.

Diversification can be achieved by investing in different asset classes, such as stocks, bonds, real estate, commodities, or cryptocurrencies. Each asset type has its own set of risks and possibilities. For example, stocks are more volatile and offer higher growth potential, while bonds are less volatile and offer more stable income. Real estate can provide both capital appreciation and rental income, while commodities can hedge against inflation and currency fluctuations. Cryptocurrencies are a new and emerging asset class that can offer high returns but also entail high risks and uncertainties.

Diversification can also be achieved by investing in different countries, industries, sizes of companies, or term lengths for income-generating investments. This way, investors can reduce the impact of specific factors that may affect one segment of the market more than others. For example, investing in different countries can reduce the exposure to political, economic, or social instability in one region. Investing in different industries can reduce the exposure to sector-specific shocks, such as technological disruption or regulatory changes. Investing in different sizes of companies can capture the growth potential of small-cap stocks and the stability of large-cap stocks. Investing in different term lengths can balance the trade-off between yield and duration risk.

The correlation coefficient between asset pairings is often used to assess the degree of diversification in a portfolio. It is a number between -1 and 1 that indicates how closely two assets move together. A correlation of -1 means that the assets move in opposite directions; a correlation of 0 means that the assets move independently, and a correlation of 1 means that the assets move in the same direction. The goal of diversification is to buy assets that have low or negative correlations with each other, so that the positive performance of some investments neutralizes the negative performance of others.

Investors can diversify their portfolios on their own by investing in select investments or holding diversified funds. Diversified funds are mutual funds or exchange-traded funds (ETFs) that invest in a basket of securities that follow an index, commodity, or sector. Diversified funds offer the benefits of diversification without the hassle of selecting and managing individual securities. However, diversified funds also have some drawbacks, such as fees, tracking errors, and lack of customization.

Diversification is a key concept in investing that can help investors achieve their financial goals while reducing their risk exposure. By spreading their capital across a range of different assets, investors can enhance their returns and lower their volatility over time.

Chapter 7

Customer-Centric Approach

A customer-centric approach is a business strategy that focuses on creating a positive experience for the customer by understanding their needs, preferences, and expectations. The goal of a customer-centric approach is to build long-term relationships with customers, increase their loyalty, and enhance their satisfaction. A customer-centric approach can benefit both customers and the businesses in various ways.

Some of the benefits of a customer-centric approach for customers are:

- They receive personalized and relevant products or services that meet their specific needs and wants.

- They enjoy seamless and consistent interaction with the business across different channels and touchpoints.
- They feel valued and appreciated by the business, which leads to increased trust and confidence.

- They have more opportunities to provide feedback and suggestions and to influence the business decisions and innovations.

Some of the benefits of a customer-centric approach for businesses are:

- They gain a deeper understanding of their customers, which helps them to anticipate their needs and expectations and to deliver superior value propositions.

- They increase their customer retention and loyalty, which reduces the cost of acquiring new customers and enhances the lifetime value of existing customers.

- They improve their customer satisfaction and advocacy, which boosts their reputation and word-of-mouth referrals.

- They foster a culture of innovation and continuous improvement, which enables them to adapt to the changing market conditions and customer demands.

To implement a customer centric approach, businesses need to adopt a customer-centric mindset and align their processes, systems, and resources with the customer perspective. Some of the steps that businesses can take to become more customer centric are:

- Conduct regular customer research and analysis, using both quantitative and qualitative methods, to gain insights into the customer segments, personas, journeys, pain points, and expectations.

- Define and communicate a clear customer-centric vision and mission, and ensure that they are shared and understood by all the employees and stakeholders.

- Design and deliver products or services that solve customer problems and create value for them, using techniques such as customer co-creation, prototyping, and testing.

- Establish and measure customer-centric metrics and key performance indicators, such as customer satisfaction, loyalty, retention, advocacy, and lifetime value, and use them to evaluate and improve the business performance and outcomes.

- Solicit and act on customer feedback and suggestions, using channels such as surveys, reviews, ratings, social media, and online communities, and show appreciation and recognition to the customers who provide them.

- Empower and train the employees to deliver excellent customer service and experience, and reward and incentivize them for doing so.

A customer-centric approach is a powerful and effective way to differentiate a business from its competitors and to create a sustainable competitive advantage. By putting the customer at the center of everything they do, businesses can not only satisfy their customers, but also delight and exceed their expectations, and build lasting and profitable relationships with them. A customer-centric approach is a continuous process that demands regular monitoring, review and improvement. Businesses that adopt a customer centric approach can expect to see positive results in terms of customer loyalty, satisfaction, advocacy and value.

Understanding Customer Need

Understanding customer needs is a crucial aspect of any successful business. Customer needs are the motivations and expectations that drive customers to purchase a product or service. By identifying and satisfying customer needs, businesses can create value for their customers, increase customer loyalty, and gain a competitive advantage.

There are different types of customer needs, such as physical, psychological, functional, emotional, social, and personal. Physical needs are the essential necessities for life, such as food, drink, shelter, and clothes.

Psychological needs are the mental and emotional factors that influence customer behavior, such as beliefs, opinions, desires, and preferences. Functional needs are the practical benefits that a product or service provides, such as solving a problem, saving time, or improving performance.

Emotional needs are the feelings that a product or service evokes, such as happiness, satisfaction, or confidence. Social needs are the influences of other people on customer decisions, such as peer pressure, social status, or belonging. Personal needs are the unique and individual factors that affect customer choices, such as personality, values, or lifestyle.

To understand customer needs, businesses need to conduct customer research and analysis. There are various methods and tools that can help businesses collect and interpret customer data, such as surveys, interviews, focus groups, observation, feedback, analytics, and segmentation. These methods can help businesses identify the needs, wants, preferences, and expectations of their target customers, as well as the gaps and opportunities in the market.

By understanding customer needs, businesses can tailor their products, services, marketing, and customer service to meet and exceed customer expectations. This can help businesses create value propositions that highlight the benefits and advantages of their offerings, as well as differentiate themselves from their competitors. Moreover, by understanding customer needs, businesses can build long-term relationships with their customers, increase customer satisfaction and retention, and generate positive word-of-mouth and referrals.

Understanding customer needs is a vital skill for any business that wants to succeed in a competitive and dynamic market. By identifying and fulfilling customer needs, businesses can create value for their customers, enhance their brand image, and achieve their business goals.

Building Customer Loyalty

Customer loyalty is the degree to which customers are satisfied with a product or service and are willing to repeat purchases and recommend it to others. It is a key indicator of customer retention and loyalty, which are essential for the success and profitability of any business. Customer loyalty can help businesses gain a loyal customer base, increase their market share, reduce their marketing and operational costs, and enhance their reputation and brand value. Therefore, building customer loyalty is a strategic goal for many businesses in today's competitive and dynamic market.

There are several strategies that can help businesses build customer loyalty, such as:

- Providing high-quality products and services that meet or exceed customer expectations and needs.

- Offering competitive prices and value propositions that demonstrate the benefits of choosing the brand over competitors.

- Creating a strong brand identity and reputation that conveys trust, credibility, and professionalism.

- Establishing a loyal customer base that can be segmented and targeted with personalized and relevant marketing campaigns and offers.

- Developing a customer-centric culture that fosters positive relationships and interactions with customers at every touchpoint.

- Encouraging customer feedback and reviews and responding to them promptly and effectively.

- Rewarding loyal customers with incentives, discounts, loyalty programs, and recognition.

- Leveraging social media and online platforms to engage with customers and build communities around the brand.

- Providing exceptional customer service and support that resolves issues and complaints quickly and satisfactorily.

- Innovating and improving the products and services based on customer feedback and market trends.

By implementing these strategies, businesses can build customer loyalty and enjoy the benefits of having a loyal and satisfied customer base. Customer loyalty can lead to increased customer retention, repeat purchases, cross-selling and up-selling opportunities, referrals, word-of-mouth, brand advocacy, and customer lifetime value. Customer loyalty can also reduce customer acquisition costs, marketing expenses, and competitive pressure. Ultimately, customer loyalty can enhance business performance and profitability and create a sustainable competitive advantage for the company.

Personalization and Customization

Personalization and customization are two terms that are often used interchangeably in the context of marketing, e-commerce, and user experience. However, they have different meanings and implications for both businesses and consumers.

Personalization refers to the process of tailoring a product, service, or experience to the individual preferences, needs, or interests of a specific user, based on the data collected about them. For example, a personalized website might show different content, recommendations, or offers to different visitors, based on their browsing history, location, or profile. Personalization aims to enhance the user's satisfaction, loyalty, and engagement, by delivering relevant and timely information or solutions.

Customization, on the other hand, refers to the process of allowing a user to modify a product, service, or experience according to their own choices or inputs. For example, a customizable website might let the user change the layout, color, or font of the interface, or select the features or options they want to use. Customization aims to empower the user and give them more control and flexibility over their experience.

Both personalization and customization have their advantages and disadvantages. Personalization can increase the user's convenience, trust, and retention, by providing a seamless and tailored experience that matches their expectations and goals. However, personalization also poses challenges such as privacy, transparency, and accuracy. Users might be concerned about how their data is collected, used, and shared, and whether they can opt out or change their preferences. Moreover, personalization algorithms might make errors or biases, or fail to capture the user's dynamic and complex needs.

Customization can enhance the user's satisfaction, autonomy, and creativity, by allowing them to express their identity and preferences, and create their own unique experience. However, customization also has drawbacks such as complexity, overload, and inconsistency. Users might be overwhelmed by the number of options or decisions they have to make, or lack the skills or knowledge to make optimal choices. Furthermore, customization might result in inconsistent or incompatible outcomes, or reduce the user's exposure to diversity or serendipity.

Personalization and customization are two different but related concepts that have different implications for the user experience. Both have their pros and cons, and the optimal balance between them depends on the context, the user, and the goal. Therefore, businesses and designers should carefully consider the trade-offs and best practices of personalization and customization, and strive to provide a user-centric and adaptive experience that meets the user's needs and wants.

Personalization and customization are two techniques that aim to enhance the customer experience by tailoring products or services to their individual needs and preferences. However, they differ in terms of who controls the changes and how they are implemented. In this essay, I will compare and contrast personalization and customization, and discuss their benefits and challenges for both customers and businesses.

Customization is the user-initiated action of modifying a product or service to meet the user's individual preferences or desires. Customization allows customers to choose the items or services they get using settings such as preferences. Customers might opt to filter the goods they see on a web browser or the emails they get. Users customize websites or applications to meet their own needs. For example, they may build shortcuts inside an application to access commonly used tools.

Personalization is the action taken by a company to create or change goods or services based on data in order to fit the preferences or wishes of consumers. It modifies the user experience by changing certain features of a product or service, such as tailoring a shop page to a customer's prior searches. Personalization, like customisation in the modification of preferences, controls changes using corporate data rather than the individual. For example, an e-commerce company may employ an algorithm to suggest more things for a consumer to buy during the checkout process.

The main difference between customization and personalization is control over the modifications. Customization enables the client or user to manage the modifications. Each consumer determines how to customize a product or service to match their own wants or expectations. In contrast, businesses and organizations have control over personalization. They determine how to develop or improve a product, service, or experience in order to better fulfill the expectations of their consumers.

Both customization and personalization have advantages and disadvantages for customers and businesses. For customers, customization can increase their satisfaction and loyalty, as they can choose what they want and how they want it. However, customization can also be overwhelming and time-consuming, as customers have to make many decisions and adjust many settings. Personalization can also increase customer satisfaction and loyalty, as it can provide relevant and tailored recommendations and communications. However, personalization can also raise privacy and ethical concerns, as customers may not be aware of how their data is collected and used.

For businesses, customization can help them differentiate themselves from competitors and increase customer retention and loyalty. However, customization can also increase the complexity and cost of production and delivery, as businesses have to accommodate many variations and options. Personalization can also help businesses differentiate themselves from competitors and increase customer retention and loyalty, as well as conversion and revenue. However, personalization can also require sophisticated technology and data analysis, as well as transparency and consent from customers.

Personalization and customization are two techniques that can improve the customer experience by tailoring products or services to their individual needs and preferences. However, they differ in terms of who controls the changes and how they are implemented. Both techniques have benefits and challenges for both customers and businesses, and they can be used together or separately depending on the context and the goals.

Feedback and Improvement

Feedback is the process of providing information to someone about their performance, behavior, or actions. Feedback can be positive, negative, or constructive, depending on the purpose and intention of the giver. Feedback can help individuals and organizations to identify their strengths and weaknesses, learn from their mistakes, and improve their skills and processes.

Improvement is the outcome of applying feedback to make changes and enhancements. Improvement can be measured by various indicators, such as quality, efficiency, productivity, customer satisfaction, profitability, and innovation. Improvement can also lead to competitive advantage, growth, and sustainability in the market.

Feedback and improvement are closely related and interdependent. Feedback without improvement is useless, as it does not lead to any change or progress. Improvement without feedback is risky, as it may not address the actual needs or expectations of the stakeholders. Therefore, feedback and improvement should be integrated and aligned in a systematic and continuous way.

One of the best practices to foster feedback and improvement in a business context is to create a culture of learning and development. This means that the organization values and encourages feedback from all sources, such as customers, employees, managers, partners, and competitors. It also means that the organization provides opportunities and resources for learning and development, such as training, coaching, mentoring, and recognition. Moreover, it means that the organization monitors and evaluates the impact of feedback and improvement on its performance and goals.

Another best practice to promote feedback and improvement in a business context is to use a feedback loop model. This is a cyclical process that involves four steps: plan, do, check, and act. In the plan step, the organization sets its objectives, strategies, and standards. In the do step, the organization implements its plans and collects data. In the check step, the organization analyzes the data and compares it with the standards. In the act step, the organization takes corrective or preventive actions based on the results and feedback. The feedback loop model helps the organization to continuously improve its quality and efficiency.

feedback and improvement are essential for business success. They help the organization to identify and address its gaps and opportunities, to learn and grow, and to achieve its goals and vision. By creating a culture of learning and development and using a feedback loop model, the organization can enhance its feedback and improvement processes and outcomes.

Chapter 8

Innovating for the Future

Innovation is essential for the future well-being of society and the economy, as it can lead to improved quality of life, increased productivity, and sustainable growth. However, innovation is not easy or automatic. It requires vision, creativity, collaboration, and perseverance. It also requires a supportive environment that fosters experimentation, learning, and adaptation. In this section, I will discuss some of the key factors that enable and challenge innovation for the future, and some of the possible solutions and opportunities that can emerge from them.

One of the main drivers of innovation for the future is the rapid advancement of technology. Technology can provide new tools, platforms, and data that can enhance the capabilities and efficiency of innovators. For example, artificial intelligence, blockchain, and quantum computing are some of the emerging technologies that have the potential to transform various domains and industries, such as health, education, finance, and energy. Technology can also enable new forms of collaboration and communication, such as online communities, crowdsourcing, and open innovation, that can tap into the collective intelligence and creativity of diverse and distributed stakeholders. Technology can also inspire new ideas and possibilities, such as virtual reality, biotechnology, and nanotechnology, that can challenge the boundaries of human imagination and experience.

However, technology also poses some significant challenges and risks for innovation for the future. Technology can create new ethical, social, and environmental dilemmas, such as privacy, security, bias, and inequality, that require careful consideration and regulation. Technology can also disrupt existing systems, structures, and norms, such as markets, institutions, and cultures, that can generate uncertainty, resistance, and conflict. Technology can also create new dependencies, vulnerabilities, and threats, such as cyberattacks, hacking, and malware, that can undermine the reliability and resilience of innovation. Therefore, technology needs to be used responsibly, inclusively, and sustainably, with a clear vision and purpose that align with the values and needs of society.

Another key factor that influences innovation for the future is the complex and dynamic nature of the problems and opportunities that innovators face. The future is characterized by uncertainty, ambiguity, and volatility, as the world is constantly changing and evolving due to various forces and trends, such as globalization, urbanization, climate change, and demographic shifts. These changes create new challenges and opportunities that require innovative solutions that are not only effective and efficient, but also adaptable and scalable. For example, the COVID-19 pandemic has exposed the fragility and interdependence of the global health, economic, and social systems, and has also stimulated the development and deployment of new vaccines, treatments, and digital platforms. Therefore, innovators need to adopt a systemic and holistic perspective that considers the multiple dimensions and implications of the problems and opportunities they address, as well as a flexible and iterative approach that allows for experimentation, feedback, and learning.

To foster and facilitate innovation for the future, it is important to create and maintain a supportive and conducive environment that enables and empowers innovators to pursue their ideas and goals. This environment consists of various elements, such as policies, resources, networks, and culture, that can influence the motivation, capacity, and impact of innovation. For example, policies can provide the legal and regulatory framework that protects and incentivizes innovation, such as intellectual property rights, tax incentives, and public funding. Resources can provide the material and human capital that supports and enhances innovation, such as infrastructure, equipment, and talent. Networks can provide the social and professional connections that enable and enrich innovation, such as mentors, partners, and customers. Culture can provide the values and norms that shape and inspire innovation, such as curiosity, openness, and diversity. Therefore, it is essential to cultivate and coordinate these elements to create a vibrant and thriving innovation ecosystem that can generate and sustain innovation for the future.

Innovation is a vital and valuable process that can create positive and lasting change for the future. However, innovation is also a challenging and complex process that requires careful and strategic management and support. By understanding and addressing the key factors that enable and challenge innovation for the future, such as technology and complexity, and by creating and maintaining a supportive and conducive environment that fosters and facilitates innovation, such as policies, resources, networks, and culture, it is possible to achieve and accelerate innovation that can benefit society and the economy in the long run.

Continuous Innovation Culture

In today's fast-paced and competitive world, organizations need to constantly innovate and improve their products, services, processes, and business models to stay ahead of the curve and meet the changing needs and expectations of their customers and stakeholders. However, innovation is not a one-time event or a sporadic activity. It is a continuous process that requires a culture that supports and encourages creativity, experimentation, learning, and collaboration. This essay will explore the concept of continuous innovation culture, its benefits, challenges, and best practices.

What is Continuous Innovation Culture?

A continuous innovation culture is a set of values, beliefs, norms, and behaviors that foster a mindset of continuous improvement and problem-solving among all members of an organization. It means that innovation is not seen as a separate function or a special project but as an integral part of everyday work and a shared responsibility for everyone. It also means that innovation is not limited to radical or disruptive ideas but encompasses incremental and evolutionary changes that can enhance the existing offerings or processes. A continuous innovation culture enables organizations to adapt to the dynamic and complex environment, generate new value propositions, and achieve sustainable competitive advantage.

Benefits of a Continuous Innovation Culture

A continuous innovation culture can bring many benefits to organizations, such as:

- Increased customer satisfaction and loyalty: By continuously innovating and improving their products and services, organizations can better meet the current and future needs and preferences of their customers and create positive and memorable experiences for them.

- Enhanced employee engagement and retention: By creating a culture of innovation, organizations can empower their employees to express their ideas, experiment with new solutions, learn from failures, and collaborate with others. This can increase their motivation, commitment, and satisfaction, and reduce turnover and absenteeism.

- Improved operational efficiency and effectiveness: By applying the principles of continuous improvement and problem-solving, organizations can eliminate waste, optimize resources, streamline processes, and reduce costs and errors.

- Higher growth and profitability: By fostering a culture of innovation, organizations can create new sources of revenue, expand their market share, differentiate themselves from competitors, and increase their profitability and sustainability.

Challenges of a Continuous Innovation Culture

Creating and sustaining a continuous innovation culture is not easy. It requires overcoming several challenges, such as:

- Resistance to change: Some people may be reluctant or fearful of changing the status quo, especially if they are comfortable with the existing routines, systems, and structures. They may perceive innovation as a threat to their roles, skills, or power, and resist or sabotage the change efforts.

- Lack of resources: Innovation requires time, money, and human capital to support the generation, evaluation, and implementation of new ideas. However, some organizations may not have sufficient or adequate resources to allocate to innovation activities, or may prioritize short-term results over long-term investments.

- Silo mentality: Some organizations may have a silo mentality, where different departments, units, or functions work in isolation and do not communicate or collaborate with each other. This can limit the flow of information, knowledge, and ideas across the organization and create barriers to innovation.

- Risk aversion: Some organizations may have a risk-averse culture where failures are not tolerated or accepted and mistakes are punished or blamed. This can discourage people from taking risks, trying new things, or learning from failures, and hinder innovation.

Best Practices for a Continuous Innovation Culture

To overcome the challenges and create a continuous innovation culture, organizations can adopt the following best practices:

- Align innovation with strategy: Organizations should align their innovation goals and initiatives with their overall vision, mission, and strategy, and communicate them clearly and consistently to all stakeholders. This can help to create a common purpose, direction, and focus for innovation, and ensure that the innovation efforts are relevant and aligned with the organizational objectives.

- Involve and empower everyone: Organizations should involve and empower all members of the organization, from top to bottom, in the innovation process, and encourage them to contribute their ideas, feedback, and suggestions. This can help to create a sense of ownership, engagement, and accountability for innovation, and leverage the diversity of perspectives, skills, and experiences within the organization.

- Create a supportive environment: Organizations should create a supportive environment that fosters creativity, experimentation, learning, and collaboration. This includes providing adequate resources, tools, and incentives for innovation, creating a safe and trusting space for people to share their ideas and opinions, celebrating successes and failures, and promoting a culture of feedback and learning.

- Implement and iterate: Organizations should implement and iterate their ideas quickly and frequently, and test them with real customers and users. This can help to validate the assumptions, hypotheses, and value propositions of the ideas, and gather feedback and data to improve and refine them. It can also help to avoid wasting time and resources on ideas that do not work or do not meet the customer's needs.

Continuous innovation culture is a key factor for organizational success in the 21st century. It can help organizations adapt to the changing environment, create new value for their customers and stakeholders, and achieve sustainable competitive advantage. However, creating and sustaining a continuous innovation culture is not easy. It requires overcoming several challenges and adopting several best practices. Organizations that can do so will be able to reap the benefits of continuous innovation and thrive in the future.

Disruptive Technology

Disruptive technology is a term coined by Harvard professor Clayton Christensen in 1995 to describe innovations that create new markets and disrupt existing ones by offering superior value to customers. Disruptive technologies often challenge the status quo and force established companies to adapt or risk losing market share. Some examples of disruptive technologies are the internet, smartphones, e-commerce, streaming services, and blockchain.

The internet is arguably the most disruptive technology in history, as it has transformed communication, information, entertainment, education, and commerce. The internet enabled the creation of new platforms and services that connected billions of people and businesses around the world. The internet also lowered the barriers to entry for entrepreneurs and innovators, who could leverage the network effects and scalability of the web to reach global audiences.

Smartphones are another example of disruptive technology, as they combine the functions of a phone, a camera, a music player, a GPS, and a computer into a single device. Smartphones revolutionized the mobile industry by offering consumers a convenient and powerful way to access the internet and various applications. Smartphones also spawned new markets and industries, such as social media, mobile gaming, ride-sharing, and mobile payments.

E-commerce is a disruptive technology that has changed the retail landscape by allowing consumers to shop online from anywhere and anytime. E-commerce challenged the traditional brick-and-mortar model by offering lower prices, a wider selection, faster delivery, and personalized recommendations. E-commerce also enabled the rise of online marketplaces, such as Amazon and Alibaba, that connected sellers and buyers across the world.

Streaming services are a disruptive technology that disrupts the media and entertainment industries by offering consumers a new way to access and consume content. Streaming services, such as Netflix and Spotify, provided consumers with unlimited and on-demand access to a vast library of movies, shows, music, and podcasts. Streaming services also bypassed the intermediaries and gatekeepers of the industry, such as cable providers, studios, and labels, and created their own original and exclusive content.

Blockchain is a disruptive technology that has the potential to transform various sectors, such as finance, the supply chain, healthcare, and governance. A blockchain is a decentralized and distributed ledger that records transactions between parties in a secure and transparent way. Blockchain eliminates the need for intermediaries and central authorities and enables peer-to-peer transactions, smart contracts, and digital assets.

Disruptive technology is a powerful force that can create new opportunities and challenges for businesses and society. Disruptive technology can offer better solutions to customer needs, create new value propositions, and generate new markets and industries. However, disruptive technology can also pose threats to incumbents, disrupt existing systems and norms, and raise ethical and regulatory issues. Therefore, it is important for business and policy leaders to understand and embrace disruptive technology and to prepare for its impact and implications.

R&D Investment

R&D investment is the amount of money that a company or an organization spends on research and development (R&D) activities. R&D activities are aimed at creating new knowledge, products, services, or processes, or improving existing ones. R&D investment is considered a key driver of innovation, competitiveness, and economic growth.

However, R&D investment is also associated with various challenges and risks, such as uncertainty, complexity, and spillovers. Uncertainty refers to the difficulty of predicting the outcomes and impacts of R&D activities, which may result in failure, waste, or obsolescence. Complexity refers to the interdependence and coordination of multiple actors, disciplines, and technologies involved in R&D activities, which may increase the costs and difficulties of managing and integrating them. Spillovers refer to the diffusion and appropriation of R&D results by other parties, which may reduce the returns and incentives for the original investors.

Therefore, R&D investment requires a careful and strategic approach that balances the benefits and costs, and considers the factors that influence its effectiveness and efficiency. Some of these factors are:

The level and type of R&D investment. Different levels of R&D investment (such as basic, applied, or experimental) and types of R&D investment (such as product, process, or organizational) may have different impacts and implications for the company and society. For example, basic research may have higher spillovers and lower returns, but also higher potential for breakthroughs and social benefits, than applied research or experimental development.

The sources and modes of R&D funding. R&D funding can come from various sources, such as internal, external, public, or private, and can be allocated in different modes, such as grants, contracts, loans, or equity. The sources and modes of R&D funding may affect the availability, stability, and direction of R&D investment, as well as the ownership, control, and sharing of R&D results.

The organization and management of R&D activities. R&D activities can be organized and managed in different ways, such as in-house, outsourced, collaborative, or open. The organization and management of R&D activities may influence the quality, quantity, and diversity of R&D inputs, outputs, and outcomes, as well as the coordination, communication, and learning among R&D actors.

The environment and context of R&D activities. R&D activities are influenced by various environmental and contextual factors, such as market conditions, technological opportunities, regulatory frameworks, social norms, and cultural values. These factors may shape the demand, supply, and direction of R&D investment, as well as the diffusion and adoption of R&D results.

R&D investment is a complex and dynamic phenomenon that requires a holistic and adaptive perspective. R&D investment can generate significant benefits for the company and society, but it also entails considerable challenges and risks. Therefore, R&D investment should be aligned with the strategic goals and capabilities of the company, and responsive to the changing needs and expectations of stakeholders.

Future Trend Analysis

Future Trends Analysis is a technique that helps organisations and individuals anticipate and prepare for the changes that are likely to occur in the near or distant future. By identifying and interpreting the patterns, drivers, and implications of various trends, future trend analysis can help create scenarios, strategies, and actions that are aligned with the desired outcomes and goals.

Future trends analysis can be applied to various domains, such as business, technology, society, the environment, and politics. Depending on the scope and purpose of the analysis, different methods and tools can be used, such as trend spotting, trend mapping, trend extrapolation, trend impact analysis, and trend forecasting.

Some of the benefits of future trend analysis are:

- It can help organizations and individuals gain a competitive edge by being proactive and innovative, rather than reactive and incremental.

- It can help organizations and individuals identify and seize new opportunities, as well as mitigate or avoid potential risks and threats.

- It can help organizations and individuals adapt to changing customer needs, preferences, and expectations, as well as emerging market dynamics and regulations.

- It can help organizations and individuals foster a culture of learning, curiosity, and creativity, as well as a mindset of resilience and agility.

Future trend analysis is not a one-time exercise, but a continuous process that requires regular monitoring, evaluation, and revision. To conduct a successful future trend analysis, **some of the steps that can be followed are:**

- Define the topic, scope, and objectives of the analysis, as well as the time horizon and the stakeholders involved.

- Collect and analyze data and information from various sources, such as academic research, industry reports, media articles, expert opinions, and social media.
- Identify and categorize the key trends that are relevant to the topic, scope, and objectives of the analysis, as well as their drivers, indicators, and impacts.

- Assess the likelihood, uncertainty, and significance of each trend, as well as the interrelationships and synergies among them.

- Create and compare different scenarios that illustrate how the trends might evolve and affect the topic, scope, and objectives of the analysis, as well as the opportunities and challenges they might create.

- Develop and prioritize strategies and actions that can help achieve the desired outcomes and goals, as well as cope with the possible contingencies and uncertainties.

- Communicate and disseminate the results and recommendations of the analysis to the relevant stakeholders, as well as solicit feedback and input for improvement.

Future trend analysis is a valuable technique that can help organizations and individuals navigate the complex and dynamic world of today and tomorrow. By using future trends analysis, organizations and individuals can become more aware, prepared, and responsive to the changes that are happening or might happen and thus shape their own future.

EVOLVE

Chapter 9
Adapting to Change

Change is inevitable in life. Whether it is a personal, professional, social, or environmental change, we all face situations that require us to adjust our attitudes, behaviors, or perspectives. Adapting to change can be challenging, but it can also be rewarding and beneficial.

The Importance of Adapting to Change

- Firstly, adapting to change can help us survive and thrive in a dynamic and uncertain world. Change can bring new opportunities, challenges, and experiences that can enrich our lives and enhance our skills. For example, learning a new language, moving to a new country, or switching careers can expose us to different cultures, perspectives, and possibilities. By adapting to these changes, we can grow as individuals and expand our horizons.

- Secondly, adapting to change can help us maintain our well-being and happiness. Change can be stressful and overwhelming, especially if it is sudden, unwanted, or negative. However, by adapting to change, we can reduce the negative impact of stress and cope with the emotions that arise from change. For example, losing a loved one, going through a divorce, or facing a health crisis can be devastating and painful. By adapting to these changes, we can accept reality, find meaning, and move forward with resilience.

- Thirdly, adapting to change can help us improve our relationships and interactions with others. Change can affect not only ourselves, but also the people around us. By adapting to change, we can communicate effectively, empathize with others, and collaborate with diverse groups. For example, working in a team, meeting new people, or resolving a conflict can require us to adapt to different personalities, opinions, and expectations. By adapting to these changes, we can build trust, rapport, and harmony with others.

The Factors that influence our ability to Adapt to change can vary depending on several factors. Some of these factors are internal, such as our personality, mindset, and values. Some of these factors are external, such as the type, frequency, and magnitude of change. These factors can either facilitate or hinder our adaptation process.

Some internal factors that can facilitate our adaptation are:

- Having a positive and optimistic outlook. This can help us see the benefits and opportunities of change, rather than the threats and losses.

- Having a flexible and open-minded attitude. This can help us embrace and accept change, rather than resist and reject it.

- Having a growth and learning orientation. This can help us seek and acquire new knowledge and skills that can help us cope with change.

- Having a purpose that is both powerful and visible. This can help us align our actions and decisions with our values and goals, regardless of the change.

Some external factors that can facilitate our adaptation are:

- Having a supportive and trustworthy network. This can help us receive and provide emotional, informational, and practical support during change.

- Having a stable and predictable environment. This can help us reduce the uncertainty and ambiguity of change, and create a sense of security and control.

- Having a gradual and manageable pace of change. This can help us adjust and adapt to change step by step, without feeling overwhelmed or rushed.

Some Strategies that Can Help Us Cope with Change

There are many strategies that can help us cope with change, but here are some of the most common and effective ones:

- Acknowledge and express your feelings. Change can trigger a range of emotions, such as fear, anger, sadness, or anxiety. It is important to acknowledge and express these feelings, rather than suppress or deny them. You can do this by talking to someone you trust, writing in a journal, or engaging in a creative activity.

- Seek and use information. Change can create a lot of confusion and doubt. It is important to seek and use information that can help you understand and deal with the change. You can do this by asking questions, doing research, or seeking feedback.

- Plan and take action. Change can create a lot of uncertainty and stress. It is important to plan and take action that can help you cope and adapt to the change. You can do this by setting realistic and specific goals, breaking down tasks into smaller steps, and monitoring your progress and results.

- Seek and use support. Change can create a lot of isolation and loneliness. It is important to seek and use support that can help you cope and adapt to the change. You can do this by reaching out to your friends, family, colleagues, or professionals who can offer you emotional, informational, or practical support.

- Take care of yourself. Change can create a lot of physical and mental strain. It is important to take care of yourself and your well-being during change. You can do this by eating well, sleeping well, exercising regularly, and engaging in activities that relax and recharge you.

Adapting to change is a vital skill that can help us survive and thrive in a changing world. Adapting to change can help us seize new opportunities, cope with stress, and improve our relationships. Our ability to adapt to change can depend on various internal and external factors. We can enhance our adaptation process by using various strategies, such as acknowledging our feelings, seeking information, planning and taking action, seeking support, and taking care of ourselves. By adapting to change, we can become more resilient, resourceful, and creative individuals.

Agility in a Dynamic Environment

The business environment today is characterized by rapid changes, uncertainty, complexity, and volatility. These conditions pose significant challenges for organizations that need to adapt and respond effectively to the shifting demands of customers, competitors, regulators, and stakeholders. To survive and thrive in such a dynamic environment, organizations need to develop and apply agility, which is the ability to renew themselves, change quickly, and succeed in a turbulent context.

Agility is not a single attribute but a multifaceted construct that can take different forms depending on the situation and the goals of the organization. According to McKinsey, agility requires two elements: a dynamic capability and a stable backbone. A dynamic capability is the ability to move fast, be nimble, and be responsive to changing conditions. A stable backbone is a platform of things that do not change, such as the core values, vision, purpose, and identity of the organization.

The stable backbone provides a foundation and a direction for the dynamic activities, while the dynamic capability enables the organization to adjust and innovate as needed.

One way to achieve agility is to adopt an organizational design that balances stability and dynamism. For example, some organizations use a dual operating system, where one part of the organization operates in a traditional hierarchical way while another part operates in a networked, fluid, and entrepreneurial way. The hierarchical part provides efficiency, reliability, and scalability, while the networked part provides creativity, experimentation, and adaptation. The two parts are aligned and integrated through shared goals, values, and processes.

Another way to achieve agility is to develop and leverage strategic agility, which is the ability to develop and quickly apply flexible, nimble, and dynamic capabilities. Strategic agility can take multiple forms, such as sensing and seizing opportunities, reconfiguring and redeploying resources, learning and unlearning, and collaborating and co-creating. These forms of strategic agility require a combination of complementary resources, skills, and competencies, such as data and analytics, innovation and entrepreneurship, leadership and culture, and partnerships and ecosystems.

The concept of agility is not a fixed condition but rather a dynamic and ongoing process that requires constant monitoring, assessment, and quality improvement. Organizations need to measure and track their agility performance using relevant indicators, such as customer satisfaction, market share, revenue growth, profitability, and employee engagement. Organizations also need to identify and address the barriers and enablers of agility, such as organizational structure, culture, processes, systems, and incentives. Organizations that can overcome the barriers and leverage the enablers of agility can gain a competitive advantage and create value in a dynamic environment.

Crisis Management

Crisis management is the act of planning for, managing, and minimizing the harm that may be caused by unanticipated, unfavorable events that occur inside an organization. The practice of predicting risks, preparing measures to reduce damage, and putting these tactics into action in the event of a crisis are all included in this discipline.

There are some characteristics that are shared by crises, regardless of the size or kind of organization: When a crisis occurs, it constitutes a danger to the firm; it involves some element of surprise, it necessitates action to alter the course of events, and it needs prompt decision-making.

It is possible for unexpected emergencies to take place when an incident takes place that is beyond the control of the organization, such as an earthquake. Alternatively, a crisis may emerge over time when a very minor issue becomes more severe as a result of the organization's failure to recognize or respond to warning indicators. Among the difficulties that fall under this category of smoldering or creeping crises are concerns about safety.

Types of crises

Crisis managers must anticipate occurrences, and knowing the main kinds of crises is a helpful preparation for building a danger list. For organizations, types of crises may relate to the region of activity or the nature of the crisis.

Natural Disaster: These crises generally result from meteorological and environmental circumstances, including storms, droughts, floods, and wildfires. Hurricane Katrina in 2005 was a noteworthy natural catastrophe.

Technological Crisis: These crises come from technological challenges such as hardware failures, software malfunctions, network problems, data loss and breaches, and computer sabotage. The transition to cloud-based storage and software as a service (SaaS) renders firms exposed to technological faults that occur at their providers. Big outages (such as a satellite or underwater data cable failure) might interrupt numerous enterprises simultaneously. The Experian data breach in 2017, in which hackers stole the personal information of over 148 million users, is an example of a technological catastrophe.

Confrontation: This form of crisis develops from confrontations between activists with a cause-related agenda and businesses or governments. These instances include boycotts, demonstrations, sit-ins, and other acts of civil disobedience. An example is environmental protestors who occupy trees to halt commercial logging.

Malevolence: This form of crisis begins with hostile or unlawful activities against a corporation, sometimes with the intention of destroying it. These acts include hacking, product tampering, industrial espionage, and executive abduction. For example, in attacks known as Night Dragon, hackers gained access to the computer networks of five major oil and gas organizations to steal confidential information.

Organizational Misdeeds: Management causes these crises when it knowingly conducts activities that damage stakeholders or crucial third parties. These activities include dishonesty, misconduct, and movements influenced by unethical or short-sighted ideas. An example of this type of tragedy happens when an executive receives a bribe to route a contract to an unqualified bidder.

Workplace Violence: These crises are attacks by an employee or former employee on other staff members at a business site due to rage tied to the attacker's employment. Other forms of violence at corporate premises against staff members, such as patients attacking healthcare providers, do not fall in this category as the attacker is not an employee or former employee.

Financial Crisis: A financial crisis could be peculiar to a company, in which a corporation has an issue like negative cash flow that limits its ability to operate. It may also be national, regional, or global, such as an economic recession that depresses sales and causes stock markets to drop. Companies respond to financial crises with short-term measures such as emergency credit lines and longer-term ones like company restructuring, layoffs, and other cost-cutting measures. The

2008 fall of Lehman Brothers due to losses accrued in the subprime mortgage industry suggests a financial disaster.

Personnel Crisis: These crises are often precipitated by the loss of significant staff members, such as a star sales representative or a genius medication inventor. These critical workers may be stolen by rivals, courted by headhunters, and lured with novel possibilities or promotions. Of course, death and retirement are factors too. Broader personnel crises emerge when worker morale falls, organizations go through times of financial crisis, and layoffs leave departments short-staffed. An example of a prospective personnel crisis occurred when Apple's Head of Design, Jony Ive, quit the corporation in 2019.

Crises can threaten the survival of an organization, harm its stakeholders, and damage its reputation. Therefore, it is essential for organizations to have a crisis management plan in place to deal with potential threats and respond effectively if they occur.

A crisis management plan is a document that outlines the roles and responsibilities of the crisis management team, the communication strategies, the risk assessment, the contingency actions, and the recovery procedures. A crisis management plan should be based on the following principles:

Prevention: The organization should identify and monitor the possible sources of crises and take proactive measures to prevent or mitigate them.

Preparedness: The organization should train and equip its staff, stakeholders, and partners to handle crises and ensure that they have access to the necessary resources and information.

Response: The organization should activate its crisis management team, communicate clearly and transparently with its internal and external audiences, and implement its contingency actions to resolve the crisis as quickly and effectively as possible.

Recovery: The organization should evaluate the impact and outcomes of the crisis, restore its normal operations, and learn from the experience to improve its future performance and resilience.

Crisis management is a vital skill for any organization that wants to survive and thrive in a complex and uncertain environment. By having a crisis management plan in place, an organization can reduce the likelihood and severity of crises, protect its reputation and stakeholder relationships, and enhance its competitive advantage and sustainability.

Leadership in Turbulent Times

Leadership is the ability to influence, inspire, and motivate others to achieve a common goal or vision. Turbulent times are periods of uncertainty, instability, and change that pose significant threats or challenges to individuals, organizations, or societies. In this segment, I will explain that leadership in turbulent times is a complex and dynamic process that requires adaptability, resilience, and creativity. I will also explore how leaders can leverage their strengths and resources to overcome the difficulties and seize the opportunities that turbulence offers.

Leaders face various challenges and opportunities in turbulent times, depending on the nature, scope, and duration of the turbulence. Some of the common challenges include dealing with ambiguity, uncertainty, and complexity; managing stress, conflict, and resistance; maintaining trust, communication, and collaboration; and balancing short-term and long-term goals. Some of the potential opportunities include learning from mistakes, feedback, and experimentation; fostering innovation, change, and growth; enhancing diversity, inclusion, and empowerment; and creating value, impact, and legacy. For example, during the COVID-19 pandemic, leaders had to cope with the unprecedented health, economic, and social crisis while also finding ways to adapt, innovate, and transform their organizations and communities.

Leaders need various skills and qualities to navigate turbulence, depending on the context, situation, and goal. Some of the essential skills and qualities include strategic thinking, decision-making, problem solving, emotional intelligence, communication, collaboration, and influence. Some of the desirable skills and qualities include creativity, innovation, agility, resilience, and learning. For example, according to a study by IBM, the most important leadership skill for the future is creativity, as it enables leaders to generate novel and useful solutions to complex and ambiguous problems.

Leaders have a significant impact and outcome on the individuals, organizations, and societies that they lead in turbulent times, depending on the actions, strategies, and values that they adopt. Some of the positive impacts and outcomes include enhancing performance, productivity, and profitability; improving morale, motivation, and engagement; fostering loyalty, trust, and commitment; and building reputation, influence, and legacy. Some of the negative impacts and outcomes include impairing quality, efficiency, and effectiveness; reducing satisfaction, well-being, and retention; creating conflict, distrust, and resentment; and damaging credibility, integrity, and ethics. For example, according to a report by McKinsey, the most successful leaders in turbulent times are those who balance empathy and clarity, resilience and agility, and purpose and pragmatism.

Leadership in turbulent times is a challenging but rewarding endeavor that requires a combination of skills, qualities, and values. Leaders who can adapt, innovate, and transform in the face of turbulence can create positive impacts and outcomes for themselves and others. However, leaders who fail to cope, learn, and grow in the midst of turbulence can cause negative impacts and outcomes for themselves and others. Therefore, it is important for leaders to develop and practice the competencies and mindsets that enable them to thrive in turbulent times. It is also essential for future research and action to explore and support the development and effectiveness of leadership in turbulent times.

Change Management Strategies

Change management strategies are the methods and practices that organizations use to plan, implement, and sustain changes in their operations, products, services, or culture. Change management strategies aim to minimize the resistance and disruption that change can cause, and to maximize the benefits and outcomes of change.

There are different models and frameworks for change management, but most of them share some common elements. Here are five steps that are essential for any effective change management process:

Define the change and its objectives. The first step is to clearly identify what is changing, why it is changing, and what are the desired results of the change. This step involves conducting a thorough analysis of the current situation, the external and internal drivers of change, the risks and opportunities of change, and the vision and goals of change. A clear and compelling definition of change can help to communicate the purpose and benefits of change to all stakeholders and to align their expectations and actions.

Assess the impact and readiness of the organization. The second step is to evaluate how the change will affect the organization and its people, processes, systems, and culture. This step involves identifying the stakeholders who will be impacted by the change, the degree and nature of the impact, the potential resistance and barriers to change, and the level of readiness and support for change. A comprehensive and realistic assessment of the impact and readiness of the organization can help to design appropriate interventions and strategies to address the gaps and challenges of change.

Develop and implement a change plan. The third step is to create a detailed and actionable plan that outlines the steps, activities, resources, roles, responsibilities, and timelines for implementing the change. This step involves defining the scope and scale of the change, the roles and responsibilities of the change team and the change agents, the communication and engagement strategies, the training and development needs, the feedback and evaluation mechanisms, and the contingency and risk management plans. A well-developed and executed change plan can help to ensure the smooth and successful implementation of the change.

Engage and communicate with stakeholders. The fourth step is to involve and inform all the stakeholders who are affected by or involved in the change. This step involves establishing and maintaining regular and transparent communication channels, providing clear and consistent messages about the change, soliciting and addressing feedback and concerns, building trust and rapport, and creating a sense of ownership and commitment among the stakeholders. Effective engagement and communication with stakeholders can help to reduce resistance and increase acceptance of the change.

Monitor and evaluate the change. The fifth step is to measure and review the progress and outcomes of the change. This step involves collecting and analyzing data and information on the performance and impact of the change, comparing the actual results with the expected results, identifying the achievements and challenges of the change, and making adjustments and improvements as needed. Continuous monitoring and evaluation of the change can help to ensure the quality and sustainability of the change.

These are the five steps in the change management process that can help any organization to plan, coordinate, and carry out change initiatives effectively. By following these steps, organizations can achieve their change objectives and enhance their performance and competitiveness in the dynamic and complex business environment.

Chapter 10

Strategic Vision

Strategic vision is an essential component of any successful organization, as it defines its long-term direction, goals, and values. A strategic vision statement is a concise and clear expression of what the organization aims to achieve or become in the future, usually within a specific timeframe. A strategic vision statement should be inspiring, realistic, unique, and aligned with the organization's mission and purpose.

The importance of strategic vision cannot be overstated, as it provides several benefits for the organization and its stakeholders. Some of these benefits are:

- It guides the strategic planning process and helps the organization set priorities, allocate resources, and measure progress.

- It motivates and empowers the employees and managers to work towards a common goal and vision and fosters a sense of ownership and commitment.

- It communicates the organization's identity and aspirations to the external stakeholders, such as customers, partners, investors, and regulators, and builds trust and credibility.

- It creates a competitive advantage for the organization as it differentiates it from its rivals and showcases its unique value proposition.

To create a strategic vision statement, the organization needs to follow a systematic and participatory process that involves the following steps:

- Conduct a situational analysis of the organization's current position, strengths, weaknesses, opportunities, and threats, as well as the external environment and trends that affect it.

- Define the organization's core values, mission, and purpose, and ensure that they are consistent and relevant.
- Identify the organization's desired future state, and articulate it in a clear and compelling way, using vivid and concrete language.

- Solicit feedback and input from the key stakeholders, such as employees, managers, customers, and partners, and incorporate their perspectives and expectations.

- Refine and revise the strategic vision statement and ensure that it is concise, coherent, and memorable.

- Communicate and disseminate the strategic vision statement to the internal and external stakeholders, and use various channels and media to convey its meaning and importance.

- Review and update the strategic vision statement periodically, and ensure that it reflects the changing realities and challenges of the organization and its environment.

A strategic vision statement is not a static document but a dynamic and living one that evolves and adapts to the organization and its context. A strategic vision statement is a powerful tool that can help the organization achieve its potential and create a positive impact on the world.

Setting Long-term Goals

Everyone has dreams and aspirations for the future, but not everyone knows how to achieve them. Setting long-term goals is a crucial step in turning your vision into reality. Long-term goals are the ones that take more than a year to accomplish, such as getting a degree, starting a business, or buying a house. They require planning, commitment, and perseverance to overcome the challenges and obstacles along the way. In this essay, I will explain how to set long-term goals, why they are important, and what benefits they can bring to your personal and professional lives.

How to Set Long-Term Goals

A good goal should be specific, measurable, achievable, relevant, and time-bound. These criteria can help you define your long-term goals clearly and realistically. For example, instead of saying "I want to be wealthy," you might say something like, "I want to save one hundred thousand dollars in five years by investing ten percent of my income every month." This goal is specific (it states the exact amount and time frame), measurable (it can be tracked and evaluated), achievable (it is within your reach and resources), relevant (it aligns with your values and interests), and time-bound (it has a deadline).

To set long-term goals, you need to have a vision of what you want to achieve in the future. You can start by asking yourself some questions, such as:

- What are my passions and interests?
- What are my strengths and skills?
- What are my values and beliefs?
- What are my needs and wants?
- What are the opportunities and threats in my environment?

These questions can help you identify your purpose, potential, and priorities. You can also use a SWOT analysis to assess your internal and external factors. A SWOT analysis is a tool that helps you analyze your strengths, weaknesses, opportunities, and threats. By doing this, you can discover your competitive advantages, areas for improvement, chances for growth, and risks to avoid.

After you have a clear vision of your desired future, you can break down your long-term goals into smaller and more manageable steps. These steps are your short-term and medium-term goals, which are the ones that take less than a year or between one and five years to achieve, respectively. For example, if your long-term goal is to get a degree in computer science, your short-term goals could be to enroll in a college, complete the required courses, and maintain a good GPA. Your medium-term goals could be to apply for internships, join extracurricular activities, and network with professors and peers.

By setting short-term and medium-term goals, you can create a roadmap for your long-term goals. You have the ability to track your progress and modify your activities appropriately. It is essential to reassess your goals on a frequent basis and to acknowledge and appreciate your progress along the way. Keeping yourself motivated, focused and confident by doing this.

Why Long-term Goals are Important

Setting long-term goals is important for several reasons.

- First, long-term goals can help you create a sense of direction and purpose in your life. They can guide your decisions and actions towards your desired outcomes. They can also help you align your personal and professional goals so that you can achieve a balance and harmony in your life.

- Secondly, long-term goals can help you develop your skills and abilities. They can challenge you to learn new things, acquire new experiences, and improve your performance. They can also help you discover your strengths and weaknesses, and work on them accordingly. By setting long-term goals, you can grow as a person and as a professional.

- Thirdly, long-term goals can help you achieve your dreams and aspirations. They can inspire you to pursue your passions and interests, and fulfill your potential. They can also help you overcome the difficulties and setbacks that you may encounter along the way. By setting long-term goals, you can make a positive difference in your life and in the lives of others.

What Benefits Long-Term Goals Can Bring

Setting long-term goals can bring many benefits to your personal and professional lives. Some of these benefits are:
- **Increased satisfaction and happiness:** Long-term goals can help you achieve your needs and wants, and improve your quality of life. They can also help you express your values and beliefs, and live authentically.

By setting long-term goals, you can increase your satisfaction and happiness in life.

- **Enhanced productivity and performance:** Long-term goals can help you organize your time and resources and prioritize your tasks and activities. They can also help you focus on your objectives and outcomes and avoid distractions and procrastination. By setting long-term goals, you can enhance your productivity and performance in your work or studies.
- **Improved self-esteem and confidence:** Long-term goals can help you recognize your achievements and accomplishments and appreciate your efforts and contributions. They can also help you cope with the challenges and failures that you may face and learn from your mistakes and feedback. By setting long-term goals, you can improve your self-esteem and confidence in yourself and your abilities.

Setting long-term goals is the key to success in life. Long-term goals are the ones that take more than a year to accomplish, such as getting a degree, starting a business, or buying a house. They require planning, commitment, and perseverance to overcome the challenges and obstacles along the way. To set long-term goals, you need to have a clear vision of what you want to achieve in the future, and break it down into smaller and more manageable steps. You also need to review your goals regularly and celebrate your achievements along the way. Setting long-term goals can help you create a sense of direction and purpose in your life, develop your skills and abilities, and achieve your dreams and aspirations. They can also bring many benefits to your personal and professional life, such as increased satisfaction and happiness, enhanced productivity and performance, and improved self-esteem and confidence. Therefore, setting long-term goals is a worthwhile and rewarding endeavor that can help you reach your full potential and make the most of your life.

Visionary Leadership

Visionary leadership is a key factor in the success of any organization, especially in today's dynamic and competitive environment. Visionary leaders have the ability to see the potential of their organization and the opportunities in the market and to align their resources and strategies accordingly. They also have the charisma and influence to inspire their followers and stakeholders to share their vision and commit to their goals.

Visionary leadership is characterized by several traits that distinguish it from other styles of leadership. Some of these traits are:

- **Forward-thinking:** Visionary leaders are always looking ahead and anticipating the future needs and expectations of their customers, employees, and society. They proactively identify potential problems and opportunities and devise effective solutions and strategies to address them. They are not satisfied with the status quo, but seek to create positive change and innovation.

- **Plan-oriented:** Visionary leaders have a clear and compelling vision of what they want to achieve and how they want to achieve it. They set SMART (specific, measurable, achievable, relevant, and time-bound) goals and objectives and communicate them clearly and consistently to their followers and stakeholders. They also monitor and evaluate their progress and performance and make adjustments as needed.

- **Effective at communicating:** Visionary leaders are skilled at conveying their vision and values to others using various channels and methods. They use storytelling, metaphors, and analogies to make their vision more vivid and appealing. They also listen actively and empathetically to their followers and stakeholders and solicit their feedback and input. They are able to adapt their communication style and message to different audiences and situations, and to overcome any barriers or resistance.

- **Optimistic:** Visionary leaders have a positive and confident attitude towards their vision and goals. They believe in their own abilities and the potential of their organization. They also instill optimism and enthusiasm in their followers and stakeholders and encourage them to overcome any challenges or difficulties. They celebrate successes and achievements and learn from failures and mistakes.

- **Creative:** Visionary leaders are not afraid to challenge conventional wisdom and assumptions and to explore new and different ways of doing things. They encourage creativity and innovation in their followers and stakeholders and foster a culture of learning and experimentation. They are open-minded and curious, and they seek to learn from diverse sources and perspectives.

Visionary leadership has many benefits for the organization and its stakeholders. Some of these benefits are:

- **Competitive advantage:** Visionary leadership enables the organization to create and sustain a competitive advantage in the market by offering unique and valuable products and services that meet or exceed the needs and expectations of the customers. Visionary leadership also helps the organization to adapt and respond quickly and effectively to the changing environment and customer preferences, seize new opportunities, and overcome new threats.

- **Employee engagement:** visionary leadership increases the level of employee engagement and satisfaction by providing them with a clear and meaningful direction, a sense of purpose, and a sense of belonging. Visionary leadership also empowers and motivates the employees to perform at their best by providing them with autonomy, recognition, and rewards. Visionary leadership also fosters a positive and supportive work environment where employees can collaborate, communicate, and learn from each other.

- **Stakeholder loyalty:** visionary leadership builds and maintains strong and trusting relationships with stakeholders, such as customers, suppliers, investors, regulators, and the community. Visionary leadership demonstrates a genuine interest and concern for the stakeholders and delivers on their promises and expectations. Visionary leadership also engages and involves the stakeholders in the vision and goals of the organization and seeks to create value and benefit for them.

Visionary leadership also faces some challenges and limitations, such as:

- **Resistance to change:** Visionary leadership may encounter resistance to change from some followers and stakeholders, who may prefer the status quo, or who may have different or conflicting interests, values, or opinions. Visionary leadership may also face opposition from competitors, who may try to undermine or sabotage their vision and goals. Visionary leadership needs to overcome these challenges by communicating the rationale and benefits of the change, addressing concerns and objections, and providing support and incentives.

- **Unrealistic expectations:** Visionary leadership may create unrealistic expectations among some followers and stakeholders, who may expect immediate or miraculous results, or who may have different or unrealistic interpretations of the vision and goals.

Visionary leadership may also have unrealistic expectations of themselves, overestimate their capabilities or resources, or underestimate the risks or difficulties. Visionary leadership needs to manage these expectations by setting realistic and attainable goals and objectives and by providing regular and honest feedback and updates.

- **Burnout:** Visionary leadership may experience burnout, due to the high level of pressure and responsibility, and the high level of commitment and dedication required to pursue their vision and goals. Visionary leaders may also neglect their own well-being and personal lives and may suffer from stress, fatigue, or health problems. Visionary leadership needs to prevent and cope with burnout, by maintaining a healthy work-life balance, delegating and sharing tasks, and seeking help and support when needed.

There are many examples of visionary leaders in the business world who have transformed their organizations and industries and who have made a positive impact on society. Some of these examples are:

- **Steve Jobs:** Steve Jobs was the co-founder and CEO of Apple, one of the most innovative and successful companies in the world. He had a vision of creating products that combined technology, design, and user experience, and that changed the way people communicate, work, and entertain. He was responsible for launching iconic products such as the Macintosh, the iPod, the iPhone, and the iPad, and for creating a loyal and passionate customer base. He was also known for his charismatic and inspiring presentation style, and for his relentless pursuit of excellence and innovation.

- **Oprah Winfrey:** Oprah Winfrey is a media mogul, philanthropist, and cultural icon. She had a vision of creating a media empire that empowered and inspired people, especially women and minorities, and addressed important social and personal issues. She was the host and producer of The Oprah Winfrey Show, one of the most popular and influential talk shows in history, and the founder and owner of Harpo Productions, a multimedia company that produces movies, books, magazines, and podcasts. She was also the founder and owner of OWN, a cable network that features diverse and uplifting content. She was also known for her generosity and compassion, and for her involvement in various charitable and educational causes.

- **Elon Musk:** Elon Musk is an entrepreneur, engineer, and visionary. He had a vision of creating a sustainable future for humanity by advancing the fields of renewable energy, space exploration, and transportation. He was the co-founder and CEO of PayPal, an online payment system that revolutionized the e-commerce industry. He was also the founder and CEO of SpaceX, a company that aims to make space travel affordable and accessible and to colonize Mars. He was also the co-founder and CEO of Tesla, a company that produces electric vehicles, batteries, and solar panels and challenges the traditional automotive industry. He was also known for his bold and ambitious ideas and for his willingness to take risks and face failures.

Visionary leadership is a vital and valuable leadership style that can help an organization achieve its goals and objectives, and create a positive impact on its stakeholders and society. Visionary leaders have the ability to see and communicate a vision for the future and to inspire and motivate others to make it a reality. They also have the skills and qualities to overcome the challenges and limitations that they may face along the way. Visionary leaders are not born, but made, and anyone can become a visionary leader, by developing and applying the traits and practices of visionary leadership.

Strategic Planning

Strategic planning is the process of defining the vision, mission, values, goals, and strategies of a business or organization. It helps to align the stakeholders around the common purpose and direction of the business, as well as to communicate the plan to the internal and external audiences. A strategic plan also serves as a roadmap to guide the actions and decisions of the business in the short and long term.

A strategic plan typically consists of the following sections:

- **Executive summary:** This is a brief overview of the main points of the strategic plan, such as the vision, mission, values, goals, and strategies. It should capture the attention and interest of the reader and highlight the unique value proposition of the business.

- **Vision statement:** This is a clear and inspiring statement of what the business wants to achieve in the future. It should reflect the aspirations and ambitions of the business, and provide a direction for the strategic plan.

- **Mission statement:** This is a concise and specific statement of the purpose and function of the business. It should describe what the business does, who it serves, and how it creates value for its customers and stakeholders.

- **Values statement:** This is a list of the core principles and beliefs that guide the behavior and culture of the business. It should reflect the values that the business wants to uphold and promote, and how it expects its employees and partners to act.

- **Environmental analysis:** This is an analysis of the internal and external elements that have an impact on the performance of the company as well as its potential. It should include a SWOT analysis, which identifies the strengths, weaknesses, opportunities, and threats of the business, as well as a PEST analysis, which examines the political, economic, social, and technological factors that influence the business environment.

- **Goals and objectives:** These are the specific and measurable outcomes that the business wants to achieve within a given time frame. They should be aligned with the vision and mission of the business, and reflect the priorities and strategies of the strategic plan. They should also be SMART, which means they should be specific, measurable, achievable, relevant, and time-bound.

- **Strategies and actions:** These are the methods and steps that the business will use to accomplish its goals and objectives. They should be based on the environmental analysis and the available resources and capabilities of the business. They should also be realistic, feasible, and flexible, and include the responsibilities, timelines, and budgets for each action.

- **Key performance indicators:** These are the metrics and indicators that the business will use to monitor and evaluate the progress and results of its strategies and actions. They should be linked to the goals and objectives of the strategic plan, and provide quantitative and qualitative data to measure the performance and impact of the business.

- **Appendix:** This is an optional section that contains any additional information or documents that support or complement the strategic plan, such as financial projections, market research, organizational charts, etc.

A strategic plan should be written in a clear, concise, and professional manner, using a business format and language. It should also be reviewed and updated regularly, to ensure that it reflects the current situation and needs of the business, and that it remains relevant and effective. A strategic plan is a valuable tool for any business that wants to achieve its vision and mission, and to grow and succeed in a competitive and dynamic market.

Sustainable Growth Strategies

Sustainable growth is the ability of a business to increase its revenue and profit over time, without compromising its social and environmental responsibilities. Sustainable growth strategies are the plans and actions that a business takes to achieve this goal, while also creating value for its stakeholders and society at large.

There are many factors that influence the sustainability of a business, such as its industry, market, competition, innovation, customer satisfaction, employee engagement, and corporate governance. However, some common elements that can help a business achieve sustainable growth are:

Integrating growth, profitability, and ESG into the core strategy. A business should align its vision, mission, and values with its growth objectives, financial performance, and environmental, social, and governance (ESG) priorities. This can help the business identify and pursue opportunities that create shared value for its customers, employees, investors, and communities, while also mitigating risks and challenges. A business that integrates growth, profitability, and ESG into its core strategy can outperform its peers in terms of revenue, profit, and shareholder returns.

Innovating ESG offerings to drive value creation. A business should leverage its core competencies and capabilities to develop and deliver products and services that address the needs and expectations of its customers while also contributing to their social and environmental well-being. This can help the business differentiate itself from the competition, enhance its brand reputation, and increase its customer loyalty and retention. A business that innovates ESG offerings to drive value creation can capture new markets, increase its market share, and improve its margins.

Using M&A to rapidly capture ESG growth pockets. A business should seek and execute strategic mergers and acquisitions (M&A) that can help it access new technologies, markets, customers, and capabilities that are aligned with its ESG goals. This can help the business accelerate its growth, diversify its portfolio, and optimize its resources and synergies. A business that uses M&A to rapidly capture ESG growth pockets can gain a competitive edge, expand its scale and scope, and increase its efficiency and effectiveness.

Tracking and reporting ESG and related data transparently. A business should measure and monitor its ESG performance and impact, using relevant indicators and standards. This can help the business evaluate its progress, identify areas for improvement, and communicate its results and achievements to its stakeholders and society. A business that tracks and reports ESG and related data transparently can enhance its accountability, credibility, and trustworthiness, while also attracting and retaining talent, customers, and investors.

Embedding strategic priorities in the organizational DNA. A business should foster a culture and mindset that support and encourage its growth, profitability, and ESG aspirations. This can help the business align its structure, processes, systems, and incentives with its strategic priorities, and empower its employees to act and collaborate accordingly. A business that embeds strategic priorities in its organizational DNA can create a cohesive and motivated workforce that drives innovation, excellence, and sustainability.

Sustainable growth strategies are essential for a business to thrive in the long term while also creating positive impacts for its stakeholders and society. By integrating growth, profitability, and ESG into the core strategy, innovating ESG offerings to drive value creation, using M&A to rapidly capture ESG growth pockets, tracking and
reporting ESG and related data transparently, and embedding strategic priorities in the organizational DNA, a business can achieve sustainable growth and success.

ADAPT

Chapter 11

Cultivating a Learning Culture

In today's rapidly changing and competitive world, organizations need to constantly adapt and innovate to stay ahead of the curve. One of the key factors that enable organizations to achieve this is cultivating a learning culture, which is an environment that encourages and supports individual and organizational learning and where knowledge acquisition and sharing of information are both appreciated and rewarded.

A learning culture can bring many benefits to an organization, such as:

- Enhancing employee engagement, retention, and loyalty, as employees feel more motivated, challenged, and supported in their personal and professional growth.

- Improving performance, productivity, and innovation, as employees acquire new skills, competencies, and perspectives that help them solve problems, create value, and seize opportunities.

- Increasing agility, resilience, and competitiveness, as employees learn how to cope with uncertainty, complexity, and change, and how to leverage their collective intelligence and creativity.

However, cultivating a learning culture is not an easy task, as it requires a strategic and holistic approach that involves multiple stakeholders and dimensions. Some of the key strategies that can help organizations create and sustain a learning culture are:

- Aiming to attract and develop agile learners, who are people that possess a growth mindset, learn from experience, question viewpoints, continue to be interested, and seek out new experiences. Agile learners are in high demand in the talent market, as they can transfer their skills and capabilities to new contexts and situations. Organizations can foster learning agility by hiring for potential, providing diverse and challenging assignments, and offering coaching and mentoring opportunities.

- Creating psychological safety, which is a climate of trust and respect, where employees feel comfortable to express their opinions, ask questions, admit mistakes, and taking risks without fear of being punished or embarrassed. Psychological safety is essential for learning, as it enables employees to experiment, learn from failures, and share feedback and ideas. Organizations can promote psychological safety by modeling and rewarding vulnerability, encouraging dissent and diversity, and addressing conflicts and errors constructively.

- Encouraging better conversations and feedback, which are the core mechanisms of learning and knowledge exchange. Conversations and feedback can help employees gain insights, perspectives, and guidance from others, as well as reflect on their own actions and outcomes. Organizations can facilitate better conversations and feedback by providing effective communication tools and platforms, training employees on how to give and receive feedback, and establishing regular and timely feedback loops.

- Making learning explicit, which means making learning visible, measurable, and aligned with the organization's goals and values. Explicit learning can help employees understand the purpose, process, and impact of their learning, as well as recognize and celebrate their achievements and progress. Organizations can make learning explicit by defining and communicating clear learning objectives and outcomes, tracking and assessing learning activities and results, and rewarding and recognizing learning efforts and accomplishments.

Cultivating a learning culture is a vital strategy for organizations to thrive in the modern world. A learning culture can enhance employee engagement, performance, and innovation, as well as increase organizational agility, resilience, and competitiveness. To create and sustain a learning culture, organizations need to attract and develop agile learners, create psychological safety, encourage better conversations and feedback, and make learning explicit.

Learning Organizations

In the modern age, businesses confront enormous problems and possibilities. The rapid pace of change, the emergence of new technologies, and the increasing complexity of the market require businesses to be agile, innovative, and adaptable. To survive and thrive in this environment, businesses need to become learning organizations.

A learning organization is an institution that encourages a culture of continual learning and knowledge development at all levels. It is an organizational paradigm that emphasizes the need for responding to change, obtaining new information, and exploiting insights to enhance performance and accomplish strategic goals. In a learning company, learning is not restricted to formal training programs or individual activities; it becomes an ingrained component of the corporate culture and processes. The whole business is involved in gaining, sharing, and using knowledge, with an emphasis on innovation, cooperation, and the capacity to adapt rapidly to problems and opportunities. Learning companies foster open communication, experimentation, and reflection, respecting the collective intellect and learning ability of their people.

There are five basic concepts or disciplines that define a learning organization.

- **Building a shared vision:** A shared vision is a fundamental quality of a learning organization that sets a common objective and has the capacity to stimulate innovation and creative thinking. When a vision is established as a team, individuals feel that their ideas are respected and that they are working towards a shared purpose.

- **Personal mastery:** Personal mastery refers to the individual's dedication and continual path toward personal development, learning, and self-improvement. It is about creating a mentality of lifelong learning and aiming for greatness in one's chosen career or area of expertise. It entails growing self-awareness, sharpening skills, and building a profound sense of purpose and desire for ongoing learning.

- **Mental models:** Mental models are the assumptions, ideas, and frameworks that form our experience and knowledge of reality. They impact how we think, behave, and connect with others. In a learning company, individuals are encouraged to question and update their mental models, to expose and test them against reality, and to adopt more accurate and effective ones.

- **Team learning:** Team learning is the process of aligning and building the ability of a team to deliver the outcomes its members actually want. It incorporates communication, cooperation, and communal problem-solving. Team learning helps the organization to tap into the different views, experiences, and abilities of its members, and to develop synergies and breakthroughs that go beyond the sum of individual contributions.

- **Systems thinking:** systems thinking is the capacity to perceive the interrelationships and patterns of change that underlie complicated situations, rather than concentrating on individual events or pieces. It is a comprehensive and dynamic way of perceiving the world and its underlying causes and effects. Systems thinking helps the company to understand the broad picture, to predict and minimize unexpected outcomes, and to utilize positive feedback loops and leverage points.

The advantages of being a learning company are varied. Learning businesses may reach improved levels of performance, creativity, and customer happiness. They can also deal better with ambiguity, complexity, and change. They may promote a culture of empowerment, involvement, and trust among their colleagues. They may also establish a competitive edge and a sustainable future for themselves and their stakeholders.

Learning organizations are a cornerstone of company success in the digital era. They are companies that embrace learning as a fundamental value and a strategic advantage. They are companies that continually learn, expand, and change with the changing environment. They are companies that are ready for the challenges and possibilities of the digital age.

Employee Development Programs

Employee Development Programs: Benefits and Best Practices

Employee development programs are efforts that attempt to strengthen the skills, knowledge, and performance of workers in a business. They may comprise many sorts of learning and development activities, such as training, coaching, mentoring, career planning, and feedback. Employee development programs are vital for firms that wish to recruit, retain, and expand their personnel, as well as fulfill their strategic objectives.

Benefits of Employee Development Programs

Employee development programs may provide various advantages for both workers and businesses, such as:

- **Increased employee engagement and satisfaction:** Employees who feel appreciated and supported by their employers are more likely to be motivated, productive, and loyal. According to a Gallup poll, workers who strongly believe that their company invests in their development are 15 times more likely to be engaged at work than those who strongly disagree.

- **Improved employee performance and productivity:** Employees who have frequent chances to learn and develop may enhance their competence and confidence, as well as apply their new skills and knowledge to their job. According to a survey by the Association for Talent Development, firms that provide comprehensive training programs had 218% greater revenue per employee and 24% larger profit margins than those that provide basic training.

- **Reduced employee turnover and recruiting costs:** Employees who have clear career pathways and growth possibilities are less inclined to quit the business or explore other positions. According to a LinkedIn poll, 94% of workers would remain at a firm longer if it invested in their professional development. Moreover, employee development programs may help organizations recruit and retain top talent, as well as decrease the costs and time involved with hiring and training new staff.

- **Enhanced organizational competitiveness and innovation:** Employees who are always learning and growing can help the firm adapt to changing market circumstances, consumer wants, and technological advances. They may also add to the organization's innovation and creativity, as well as its reputation and brand image. According to a report by PwC, 77% of CEOs feel that the availability of vital talents is the largest danger to their company's success.

Best Practices for Employee Development Programs

To design and implement effective employee development programs, organizations should follow some best practices, such as:

- **Align employee development with organizational goals and values:** Employee development programs should be aligned with the organization's vision, mission, values, and strategic objectives. They should also reflect the organization's culture and learning philosophy, as well as the needs and expectations of its stakeholders.

- **Assess employee needs and interests:** Employee development programs should be based on a thorough assessment of the current and future skills and knowledge gaps of the employees, as well as their career aspirations and preferences. Organizations can use various methods to assess employee needs and interests, such as surveys, interviews, performance reviews, and feedback.

- **Provide diverse and flexible learning opportunities:** Employee development programs should offer a variety of learning and development activities that cater to different learning styles, preferences, and levels. They should also provide flexible and accessible learning options that suit the employees' schedules, locations, and pace. Organizations can use a blended learning approach that combines online and offline, formal and informal, and individual and collaborative learning methods.

- **Support and monitor employee development:** Employee development programs should be supported by adequate resources, such as budget, time, technology, and mentors. They should also be monitored and evaluated regularly to measure their effectiveness, impact, and return on investment. Organizations can use various tools and metrics to track and analyze employee development, such as learning management systems, feedback, and analytics.

Employee development programs are vital for organizations that want to achieve their strategic goals and enhance their competitiveness and innovation. By investing in the skills, knowledge, and performance of their employees, organizations can increase their engagement, productivity, and retention. However, employee development programs should not be seen as a one-size-fits-all solution. Organizations should align their programs with their goals and values, assess their employees' needs and interests, provide diverse and flexible learning opportunities, and support and monitor their progress. By doing so, they can ensure that their programs are effective, impactful, and beneficial for both the employees and the organization.

Knowledge Sharing Initiatives

Knowledge sharing is the act of providing space for open discussion about the victories, losses, and lessons that workers are jointly experiencing in the workplace. It is essential for enhancing productivity, innovation, and trust among the team members. It also helps to nurture the organization's knowledge bank so that everyone can access it, even as people come and go. However, knowledge sharing is not always easy or natural for employees. It requires a supportive environment, effective leadership, and appropriate incentives to foster a culture of learning and collaboration.

One of the key factors in creating a knowledge-sharing culture in the organization is to establish a clear vision and purpose for knowledge-sharing. Employees need to understand why knowledge sharing is important for the organization's success and how it can benefit them personally and professionally. Moreover, employees need to feel comfortable and safe to share their knowledge without fear of criticism, judgment, or losing their competitive edge. Therefore, the organization should foster a climate of trust, respect, and openness among the team members, where knowledge sharing is valued and appreciated. Some of the activities and practices that can promote a culture of knowledge sharing are:

- Creating a common platform or repository where employees can easily access and contribute to the organization's knowledge bank. This can be done using online tools such as wikis, blogs, forums, or intranets, where employees can share their insights, experiences, best practices, or lessons learned.

- Encouraging informal and formal interactions among employees across different levels, functions, and locations. This can be done by organizing events such as workshops, seminars, webinars, or social gatherings, where employees can exchange ideas, feedback, or advice on various topics or projects.

- Providing opportunities for employees to learn from each other and from external experts. This can be done by facilitating mentoring, coaching, or peer-to-peer learning programs, where employees can seek or offer guidance, support, or expertise to their colleagues or mentors. Alternatively, the organization can invite external speakers, consultants, or trainers to share their knowledge and skills with the employees.

Another important factor for encouraging knowledge sharing in the organization is to provide effective leadership and rewards for knowledge sharing behaviors. Employees need to see that their leaders value and practice knowledge sharing themselves, and that they support and recognize the employees who share their knowledge with others. Therefore, the organization should develop and communicate a clear vision and strategy for knowledge sharing, and align it with the organization's goals and values. Some examples of how leaders can encourage and reward knowledge sharing are:

- Modeling and demonstrating knowledge-sharing behaviors by sharing their own knowledge, asking for feedback, and acknowledging the contributions of others.
- Providing guidance and coaching to employees on how to share knowledge effectively, such as using appropriate tools, formats, and channels.

- Creating and facilitating opportunities for employees to share knowledge with each other and with external stakeholders, such as customers, partners, or suppliers.
- Providing positive and constructive feedback to employees on their knowledge sharing efforts, and celebrating their successes and achievements.
- Offering incentives and rewards for knowledge sharing, such as recognition, praise, bonuses, promotions, or career development opportunities.

Despite the benefits of knowledge sharing, there are also some challenges and barriers that can hinder its effectiveness in the workplace. Some of the common challenges and barriers are:

- Lack of time and resources to share knowledge effectively. Employees may be too busy or overwhelmed with their own tasks and deadlines to spend time sharing or seeking knowledge from others.

- Fear of losing competitive advantage or job security by sharing knowledge.

Employees may perceive knowledge as a scarce and valuable resource that gives them an edge over others and may be reluctant to share it with potential competitors or newcomers.

- Low awareness or appreciation of the value of knowledge. Employees may not realize the benefits of knowledge sharing for themselves, their colleagues, or the organization, and may not see it as a priority or a responsibility.

- Poor communication and collaboration skills or tools. Employees may lack the skills or tools to share knowledge effectively, such as writing, speaking, listening, or using online platforms or repositories.

- Cultural and linguistic differences among employees. Employees may have different backgrounds, values, beliefs, or languages that affect their willingness or ability to share knowledge with others who are different from them.

- Unsupportive organizational culture or leadership. Employees may face resistance or discouragement from the organizational culture or the leadership that does not value or reward knowledge sharing, or that creates a climate of distrust, competition, or hierarchy.

To overcome these challenges and barriers, the organization should implement some strategies and solutions, such as:

- Providing sufficient time and resources for knowledge sharing activities, such as allocating dedicated time slots, creating knowledge sharing budgets, or reducing workload pressures.

- Creating a culture of trust and openness where employees feel safe and comfortable to share their knowledge without fear of negative consequences and where knowledge sharing is recognized and appreciated.

- Raising awareness and education on the value and importance of knowledge sharing, such as communicating the vision and goals of knowledge sharing, highlighting the benefits and success stories, or providing training and coaching on knowledge sharing skills and tools.

- Improving communication and collaboration tools and platforms, such as adopting user-friendly and accessible online tools, creating common standards and formats, or providing technical support and feedback.

- Respecting and embracing diversity and inclusion, such as promoting cross-cultural and cross-functional interactions, providing language support or translation, or celebrating different perspectives and experiences.

- Developing and communicating supportive policies and practices, such as establishing clear roles and responsibilities, providing incentives and rewards, or involving and empowering employees in decision making and problem solving.

Knowledge sharing is a vital process for enhancing the performance and innovation of the organization and its employees. However, knowledge sharing is not always easy or natural for employees, and it requires a supportive environment, effective leadership, and appropriate incentives to foster a culture of learning and collaboration.

Continuous Training

Continuous training is the process of providing employees with ongoing learning opportunities to enhance their skills and knowledge. It can take various forms, such as formal courses, informal learning, coaching, mentoring, shadowing, and self-directed learning. Continuous training is essential for businesses to stay competitive and adaptable in a rapidly changing world.

There are many benefits of continuous training for both businesses and employees. Some of the benefits for businesses are:

- **Improved performance and productivity:** Continuous training helps employees perform their tasks more efficiently and effectively, leading to better outcomes and higher customer satisfaction. Continuous training also helps employees keep up with the latest industry trends and best practices, ensuring that they deliver high-quality products and services.

- **Competitive advantage:** Continuous training gives businesses an edge over their competitors, as they can offer more innovative and customized solutions to their customers. Continuous training also helps businesses attract and retain top talent, as employees value learning and development opportunities.

- **Cost-effectiveness:** Continuous training can reduce costs associated with employee turnover, recruitment, and retraining. Continuous training can also prevent errors, mistakes, and accidents that can result in losses and liabilities.

- **Customer loyalty:** Continuous training enables employees to provide excellent customer service and build strong relationships with customers. Continuous training also helps employees anticipate and meet customer needs and expectations, resulting in higher customer retention and referrals.

Some of the benefits for employees are:

- **Career progression:** Continuous training helps employees advance their careers by acquiring new skills and qualifications. Continuous training also helps employees demonstrate their value and potential to their employers, increasing their chances of promotion and recognition.

- **Professional confidence:** Continuous training boosts employees' confidence and self-esteem, as they feel more competent and capable in their roles. Continuous training also helps employees overcome challenges and solve problems, enhancing their critical thinking and creativity.

- **Skill sharing:** Continuous training fosters a culture of collaboration and knowledge sharing among employees, as they learn from each other and exchange feedback.

Continuous training also helps employees develop their communication and interpersonal skills, improving their teamwork and cooperation.

- **Personal enrichment:** Continuous training enriches employees' personal and professional lives, as they learn new things and discover new interests. Continuous training also helps employees achieve their personal and professional goals, increasing their motivation and satisfaction.

To implement continuous training effectively, businesses need to follow some best practices, such as:

- **Assess learning gaps:** Businesses need to identify the current and future skills and knowledge gaps of their employees, and design training programs that address them. Businesses can use various methods, such as surveys, interviews, tests, and performance reviews, to assess learning gaps.

- **Get a team on board:** Businesses need to involve their employees in the planning and implementation of continuous training, and communicate the benefits and expectations clearly. Businesses can also solicit feedback and suggestions from their employees and incorporate them into their training programs.

- **Use a learning management system:** Businesses need to use a learning management system (LMS) to deliver, manage, and track continuous training. An LMS can help businesses create, store, and distribute various types of learning content, such as courses, videos, articles, and quizzes. An LMS can also help businesses monitor and measure the effectiveness and impact of continuous training, using data and analytics.

- **Encourage learning while doing:** Businesses need to provide employees with opportunities to apply their learning to their work, and reinforce their learning through practice and repetition. Businesses can also use gamification, simulations, and scenarios to make learning more engaging and realistic.

- **Customize learning experiences:** Businesses need to tailor continuous training to the needs, preferences, and goals of their employees, and offer them flexibility and autonomy in their learning. Businesses can also use adaptive learning, which adjusts the difficulty and pace of learning based on the learner's performance and progress.

- **Create a peer-to-peer learning network:** Businesses need to encourage and facilitate peer-to-peer learning among employees, and create a supportive and collaborative learning environment. Businesses can also use social learning, which leverages social media, forums, blogs, and chats, to enable employees to share their learning and insights with each other.

- **Reward learning:** Businesses need to recognize and reward employees for their learning achievements and efforts, and provide them with incentives and feedback. Businesses can also use badges, certificates, and points to acknowledge and motivate employees for their learning.

Continuous training is a key to business success, as it helps businesses and employees stay relevant, competitive, and adaptable in a fast-changing world. Continuous training also helps businesses and employees improve their performance.
Productivity, and satisfaction, and achieve their goals and objectives. Therefore, businesses should invest in continuous training and make it a part of their culture and strategy.

Chapter 12

Mentoring and Coaching

Mentoring and coaching are two related but distinct processes that aim to enhance the performance, skills, and potential of individuals or teams in a business context. Mentoring is a long-term, developmental relationship between a senior and a junior, where the mentor provides guidance, advice, and support to the mentee. Coaching is a short-term, goal-oriented intervention that focuses on improving specific competencies or behaviors of the coachee, usually with the help of a professional coach.

Both mentoring and coaching can offer significant benefits for businesses, such as:

- Increased employee engagement, retention, and loyalty: Mentoring and coaching can foster a sense of belonging, recognition, and appreciation among employees, as well as provide them with opportunities for personal and professional growth. This can enhance their motivation, commitment, and satisfaction with their work and the organization.

- Enhanced performance, productivity, and innovation: Mentoring and coaching can help employees develop new skills, knowledge, and perspectives, as well as overcome challenges, solve problems, and achieve goals. This can boost their confidence, competence, and creativity, leading to improved outcomes and results.

- Strengthened organizational culture and values: Mentoring and coaching can promote a culture of learning, feedback, and collaboration within the organization, as well as align the behaviors and actions of employees with the vision, mission, and values of the business.

To implement an effective mentoring and coaching strategy, businesses should consider the following steps:

- Define the objectives and scope of the mentoring and coaching program: Businesses should identify the purpose, goals, and expected outcomes of the program, as well as the target audience, duration, and frequency of the sessions.

- Select and train the mentors and coaches: Businesses should choose qualified and experienced mentors and coaches who have the relevant skills, knowledge, and personality to work with the mentees and coachees. They should also provide them with adequate training, resources, and support to perform their roles effectively.

- Match the mentees and coachees with the mentors and coaches: Businesses should use a systematic and transparent process to pair the mentees and coachees with the mentors and coaches, based on their needs, preferences, and compatibility. They should also ensure that both parties agree on the expectations, roles, and responsibilities of the relationship.

- Monitor and evaluate the progress and impact of the mentoring and coaching program: Businesses should collect and analyze data and feedback from the participants and stakeholders of the program, such as the mentors, coaches, mentees, coachees, managers, and customers. They should also use the results to measure the effectiveness, efficiency, and quality of the program, as well as to identify the strengths, weaknesses, and areas for improvement.

Mentoring and coaching are powerful tools that can help businesses achieve their objectives and enhance their competitive advantage. By investing in the development and empowerment of their employees, businesses can foster a culture of excellence, innovation, and growth.

Harnessing Mentorship

Mentorship is a partnership in which a more experienced or knowledgeable person help to assist a less experienced or less knowledgeable person. Mentorship can be a powerful tool for enhancing the performance, productivity, and satisfaction of employees and organizations. In this essay, I will discuss the benefits of mentorship, the challenges of implementing it, and the best practices for harnessing its potential.

Benefits of Mentorship

Mentorship can bring many benefits to both the mentors and the mentees, as well as the organization as a whole. Some of the benefits are:

- **Knowledge transfer:** Mentorship can facilitate the transfer of knowledge, skills, and expertise from experienced employees to new ones, ensuring a smooth transition and faster onboarding. Mentorship can also foster a culture of learning and innovation, as mentors and mentees can exchange ideas and feedback.

- **Employee development:** Mentorship can provide a structured framework for employee development, as mentors can help mentees set goals, monitor progress, and provide support and guidance. Mentorship can also enhance the confidence, motivation, and self-awareness of mentees, as they can learn from the successes and failures of their mentors.

- **Employee retention:** Mentorship can increase the loyalty and commitment of employees, as they can feel valued and supported by the organization. Mentorship

can also reduce the turnover rate, as employees can have more opportunities for career advancement and personal growth.
- **Organizational performance:** Mentorship can improve organizational performance as employees can work more effectively and efficiently, with higher quality and lower costs. Mentorship can also foster a positive and collaborative work environment, as employees can build trust and rapport with each other.

Challenges of Mentorship

Despite the benefits of mentorship, there are also some challenges that need to be addressed to ensure its success. Some of the challenges are:

- **Matching:** Finding the right match between mentors and mentees can be difficult, as there may be differences in personality, style, expectations, and goals. A mismatch can lead to frustration, conflict, and dissatisfaction for both parties.

- **Commitment:** Maintaining a consistent and meaningful mentorship relationship can be challenging, as both mentors and mentees may have competing demands and priorities. A lack of commitment can result in a loss of interest, engagement, and trust for both parties.

- **Evaluation:** Measuring the impact and outcomes of mentorship can be challenging, as there may be no clear or objective indicators of success. A lack of evaluation can result in a lack of accountability, feedback, and improvement for both parties.

Best Practices for Harnessing Mentorship

To overcome the challenges and maximize the benefits of mentorship, there are some best practices that can be followed by both the organization and the individuals involved. Some of the best practices are:

- **Planning:** The organization should have a clear and comprehensive plan for implementing and managing the mentorship program, including the objectives, scope, criteria, process, roles, responsibilities, and resources. The plan should also be aligned with the organizational vision, mission, and values.

- **Training:** The organization should provide adequate and appropriate training for both mentors and mentees, covering the skills, techniques, and tools needed for effective mentorship. The training should also address the potential issues and challenges that may arise during the mentorship relationship.

- **Support:** The organization should provide ongoing and timely support for both mentors and mentees, including the recognition, feedback, and incentives. The support should also include the provision of a mentorship coordinator or facilitator, who can oversee and monitor the mentorship program and intervene when necessary.

- **Evaluation:** The organization should conduct regular and systematic evaluation of the mentorship program, using both quantitative and qualitative methods. The evaluation should measure the inputs, outputs, and outcomes of the mentorship program, as well as the satisfaction and feedback of both mentors and mentees.

Mentorship is a key strategy for business success, as it can bring many benefits to both the employees and the organization. However, mentorship also poses some challenges that need to be addressed to ensure its effectiveness and sustainability. By following the best practices of planning, training, support, and evaluation, the organization can harness the potential of mentorship and achieve its goals.

Coaching for Success

Coaching is the process of facilitating learning and development in individuals or groups to help them achieve their personal or professional goals. Coaching can be applied in various contexts, such as life coaching, executive coaching, career coaching, sports coaching, and more. In this essay, I will focus on the benefits and challenges of coaching for success in a business setting.

Benefits of Coaching for Success

Coaching for success can bring many advantages to both the coach and the coachee, as well as the organization they belong to. Some of the benefits are:

- Coaching can enhance the performance and productivity of the coachee by helping them identify their strengths, weaknesses, opportunities, and threats, and develop action plans to improve their skills and competencies.

- Coaching can increase the motivation and engagement of the coachee by providing them with feedback, recognition, support, and encouragement, and by aligning their goals with the organizational vision and values.

- Coaching can foster the personal and professional growth of the coachee by facilitating self-awareness, self-confidence, self-regulation, and self-efficacy, and by encouraging them to take responsibility for their own learning and development.

- Coaching can improve the communication and collaboration of the coachee by enhancing their listening, questioning, and interpersonal skills, and by building trust and rapport with the coach and other stakeholders.

- Coaching can create a positive and learning-oriented culture in the organization by promoting a growth mindset, a feedback culture, a continuous improvement mentality, and a shared vision and purpose.

Challenges of Coaching for Success

Coaching for success can also pose some challenges and difficulties for both the coach and the coachee, as well as the organization they belong to. Some of the challenges are:

- Coaching can be time-consuming and resource-intensive, as it requires regular and frequent sessions, follow-ups, assessments, and evaluations, and it may involve additional costs for training, materials, and tools.

- Coaching can be complex and dynamic, as it depends on various factors, such as the coach's and the coachee's personalities, styles, preferences, expectations, and readiness, as well as the organizational context, culture, and climate.

- Coaching can be challenging and uncomfortable, as it may involve confronting difficult issues, giving and receiving constructive feedback, dealing with resistance and conflict, and overcoming barriers and obstacles.

- Coaching can be risky and uncertain, as it may not guarantee the desired outcomes, results, or impacts, and it may face ethical dilemmas, confidentiality issues, or legal implications.

Coaching for success is a powerful and effective way of enhancing the performance, motivation, growth, and communication of individuals and groups in a business setting. However, coaching for success also entails some challenges and difficulties that need to be addressed and overcome. Therefore, coaching for success requires a high level of competence, commitment, and collaboration from both the coach and the coachee, as well as the support and involvement of the organization.

Peer Learning Groups

In today's complex and dynamic business environment, leaders need to constantly update their skills and knowledge to cope with the challenges and opportunities they face. However, traditional methods of learning, such as lectures, workshops, or online courses, may not be enough to meet the diverse and evolving needs of leaders. Therefore, there is a need for more innovative and effective ways of learning that can foster collaboration, feedback, and problem-solving among leaders.

One such way is peer learning groups, which are small groups of leaders who meet regularly to share their experiences, insights, and perspectives on various topics related to their work. Peer learning groups are based on the premise that leaders can learn from each other, as well as from experts or instructors, by engaging in active and social learning processes. Peer learning groups can offer several benefits for leadership development, such as:

- **Teamwork:** Peer learning groups can help leaders develop their teamwork, cooperation, and communication skills, as they have to work with others who may have different backgrounds, opinions, and styles. Peer learning groups can also create a sense of community and support among leaders, which can enhance their motivation and engagement in learning.

- **Feedback:** Peer learning groups can provide leaders with constructive and timely feedback, which can help them identify their strengths and areas for improvement. Peer feedback can also help leaders gain a more accurate and balanced view of their performance and impact, as well as learn from the best practices and mistakes of others.

- **Diversity:** Peer learning groups can expose leaders to diverse perspectives, experiences, and challenges, which can broaden their horizons and stimulate their creativity and innovation. Peer learning groups can also help leaders appreciate and leverage the diversity of their teams and organizations, as well as understand and adapt to different cultures and contexts.

- **Application:** Peer learning groups can help leaders apply their learning to real-world situations, as they can discuss and analyze relevant and current issues and problems that they face in their work. Peer learning groups can also help leaders transfer their learning to their teams and organizations, as they can share their insights and solutions with others and implement them in practice.

To create and sustain effective peer learning groups, there are some key factors that need to be considered, such as:

- **Purpose:** Peer learning groups should have a clear and shared purpose, which defines the goals, objectives, and expectations of the group. The purpose should also align with the individual and organizational needs and priorities of the leaders.

- **Structure:** Peer learning groups should have a well-defined structure, which specifies the size, composition, frequency, duration, and format of the group meetings. The structure should also ensure that the group meetings are organized, focused, and productive, and that the group members have equal opportunities to participate and contribute.

- **Facilitation:** Peer learning groups should have a skilled and supportive facilitator, who can guide and moderate the group discussions, as well as provide relevant and useful resources and materials. The facilitator should also encourage and foster a positive and respectful learning climate, where the group members can trust, challenge, and learn from each other.

Peer learning groups are a valuable strategy for leadership development, as they can offer leaders multiple benefits, such as teamwork, feedback, diversity, and application. However, to make the most of peer learning groups, leaders need to consider the purpose, structure, and facilitation of the groups, and commit to their active and continuous participation and improvement. By doing so, leaders can enhance their learning outcomes and performance, as well as the learning culture and effectiveness of their teams and organizations.

Leadership Development

Leadership development is the process of strengthening the leadership skills of any member of an organization. It involves honing, developing, and effectively applying key skills such as influence, strategic thinking, delegation, coaching and mentoring, executive presence, and more. Leadership development is important for businesses because it can improve performance, innovation, employee engagement, and organizational culture.

How Leadership Development can be Achieved.

One of the essential aspects of leadership development is acquiring and enhancing the skills that enable leaders to effectively lead themselves and others. Some of the key skills that leaders need are communication, decision-making, problem-solving, creativity, and emotional intelligence. Communication skills allow leaders to articulate their vision, goals, and expectations clearly and persuasively, as well as listen actively and empathetically to feedback and concerns. Decision-making skills help leaders to analyze situations, weigh alternatives, and choose the best course of action. Problem-solving skills enable leaders to identify and resolve issues, overcome obstacles, and implement solutions. Creativity skills foster the ability of leaders to generate new ideas, innovate, and adapt to changing circumstances. Emotional intelligence skills empower leaders to understand and manage their own emotions, as well as recognize and influence the emotions of others.

Another important aspect of leadership development is applying and refining the strategies that help leaders to achieve their objectives and optimize their performance. Some of the common strategies that leaders use are goal-setting, delegation, coaching, and mentoring. Goal-setting is the process of defining and prioritizing specific, measurable, achievable, relevant, and time-bound goals that align with the organizational vision and mission. Delegation is the act of assigning and empowering others to perform tasks and responsibilities that match their skills and interests. Coaching is the practice of providing guidance, feedback, and support to help others improve their skills and achieve their goals. Mentoring is the act of sharing knowledge, experience, and advice with less experienced or aspiring leaders.

The third aspect of leadership development is realizing and maximizing the benefits that leadership development brings to individuals, teams, and organizations. Some of the benefits of leadership development are improved performance, increased engagement, enhanced collaboration, and greater resilience. Improved performance means that leaders and their followers can deliver better results, quality, and efficiency. Increased engagement means that leaders and their followers can feel more motivated, committed, and satisfied with their work. Enhanced collaboration means that leaders and their followers can work together more effectively, harmoniously, and productively. Greater resilience means that leaders and their followers can cope with stress, adversity, and change more positively and proactively.

Leadership development is a vital process for any member of an organization who wants to lead effectively and efficiently. Leadership development involves acquiring and enhancing skills, applying and refining strategies, and realizing and maximizing benefits. By developing their leadership abilities, leaders can improve their own performance, increase their followers' engagement, enhance their collaboration, and foster their resilience. Leadership development is not only beneficial for individuals and teams but also for the entire organization and society. Therefore, I recommend that businesses invest more in leadership development programs and initiatives, and that aspiring and current leaders seek more opportunities to learn and grow as leaders.

Chapter 13

Embracing Failure

Failure is often seen as something to be avoided or feared in the business world. Many businesses strive for perfection and success and view failure as a sign of incompetence or weakness. However, this attitude can limit the potential of businesses to grow, innovate, and excel in a competitive and dynamic market.

One of the benefits of embracing failure is that it can help businesses identify their weaknesses, improve their performance, and adapt to changing environments. Failure can serve as a feedback mechanism that reveals the gaps or flaws in a business's strategy, product, or service. By analyzing the causes and consequences of failure, businesses can learn from their mistakes and make necessary adjustments or corrections. For example, Apple learned from its failure with the Newton device, a personal digital assistant that was too expensive and had poor handwriting recognition, and later created the successful iPhone, a smartphone that revolutionized the industry. Similarly, Toyota used the concept of "intelligent failure" to improve its quality and efficiency. The company encouraged its employees to experiment with new ideas and processes, and report any failures or problems as soon as possible. This way, Toyota could quickly identify and solve any issues, preventing them from escalating or recurring. Failure can also help businesses cope with uncertainty and volatility in the market. By embracing failure, businesses can become more resilient, flexible, and ready to face new challenges or opportunities.

Another benefit of embracing failure is that it can foster a culture of experimentation, creativity, and risk-taking in businesses. Failure can encourage businesses to try new ideas, methods, or solutions, and not be afraid of making mistakes or facing challenges. By experimenting with different possibilities, businesses can discover new opportunities, markets, or customers and create innovative products or services that meet their needs. For example, 3M discovered the adhesive for Post-it notes by accident, when a scientist failed to create a strong glue and instead produced a weak one that could be easily removed. Similarly, Netflix pivoted from a DVD rental service to a streaming platform after facing bankruptcy, and became one of the most successful and influential media companies in the world. Failure can also stimulate creativity and originality in businesses, as they can learn from their failures and generate new ideas or solutions that are better than the previous ones. For instance, Dyson invented the world's first bagless vacuum cleaner after failing more than 5,000 prototypes. Failure can also promote risk-taking and courage in businesses, as they can overcome their fear of failure and pursue their goals with confidence and determination. For example, Airbnb faced many rejections and challenges before becoming a global phenomenon, but the founders never gave up and took risks to grow their business.

However, embracing failure is not without its challenges or drawbacks. Failure can also have negative impacts on businesses, such as losing customers, reputations, or resources. Failure can damage the trust and loyalty of customers, especially if the failure affects the quality, safety, or reliability of the product or service. For example, Boeing faced a huge crisis after two fatal crashes involving its 737 Max jets, which resulted in a loss of orders, revenue, and reputation. Failure can also harm the image and credibility of a business, especially if the failure is due to ethical, legal, or social issues. For example, Volkswagen suffered a scandal after admitting to cheating on emissions tests, which led to lawsuits, fines, and public outrage. Failure can also consume the time, money, and energy of a business, especially if the failure is repeated or prolonged. For example, Quibi, a short-form video streaming service, shut down after only six months of operation, after failing to attract enough subscribers and advertisers.

Therefore, businesses should not embrace failure blindly or recklessly, but rather manage it effectively and minimize its negative impacts. Some strategies or best practices for doing so are: having a clear vision and purpose, setting realistic and measurable goals, learning from feedback, and celebrating small wins. These can help businesses stay focused, motivated, and accountable, and avoid repeating the same mistakes, blaming others, or giving up easily. Businesses should also balance the risks and rewards of failure, and know when to persist, pivot, or quit. These can help businesses optimize their resources, adapt to changing circumstances, and seize new opportunities.

Failure is not something to be feared or avoided, but rather embraced and utilized as a source of learning and innovation. I have shown how failure can help businesses identify their weaknesses, improve their performance, and adapt to changing environments. I have also discussed how failure can foster a culture of experimentation, creativity, and risk-taking in businesses. However, I have also acknowledged the potential challenges or drawbacks of embracing failure, and suggested some strategies or best practices for managing failure effectively and minimizing its negative impacts. Therefore, I recommend that businesses should adopt a positive and constructive approach to failure, and see it as an opportunity to grow, innovate, and excel. By doing so, businesses can achieve greater success and satisfaction in the long run.

Learning from Mistakes

Mistakes are inevitable in any human endeavor, especially in the complex and dynamic world of business. However, mistakes are not necessarily bad, as long as they are recognized, corrected, and learned from. In fact, learning from mistakes can be a powerful source of innovation, improvement, and competitive advantage for any organization.

Learning from mistakes requires a culture of psychological safety, where people feel comfortable to speak up, admit errors, and ask for help without fear of being blamed or punished. In such a culture, mistakes are seen as opportunities to learn and grow, rather than as failures to be avoided or hidden. Edmondson argues that psychological safety fosters a learning orientation, where people are motivated to seek feedback, experiment, and reflect on their actions and outcomes.

Learning from mistakes also requires a systematic process of identifying, analyzing, and resolving errors. One such process is the After Action Review (AAR), which was developed by the U.S. Army and has been adopted by many organizations in different sectors. An AAR is a structured debriefing session that involves four questions: What was supposed to happen? What actually happened? Why did it happen? What can we do better next time? By answering these questions, participants can share their perspectives, learn from each other, and generate actionable insights and recommendations for improvement.

Learning from mistakes can have several benefits for businesses, such as:

- **Enhancing creativity and innovation:** Mistakes can stimulate new ideas and solutions, as well as encourage experimentation and risk-taking. For example, the invention of the Post-it note was a result of a failed attempt to create a strong adhesive.

- **Improving performance and quality:** Mistakes can reveal gaps in knowledge, skills, processes, or systems, and provide feedback for improvement. For example, Toyota's famous production system is based on the principle of continuous improvement through identifying and eliminating errors.

- **Building trust and resilience:** Mistakes can foster a culture of openness, honesty, and accountability, as well as strengthen the ability to cope with challenges and failures. For example, Netflix's CEO Reed Hastings publicly admitted and apologized for a major strategic mistake in 2011 and managed to regain the trust and loyalty of his customers and employees.

Steps to Take When a Mistake Occurs

When a mistake occurs, the following steps can help businesses to learn from it effectively:

- **Acknowledge and accept the mistake:** The first step is to admit the mistake, take responsibility for it, and avoid blaming others or making excuses. This can help to reduce the negative emotions and defensiveness that often accompany mistakes, and create a safe and supportive environment for learning.

- **Analyze and understand the mistake:** The next step is to examine the mistake, identify the root causes, and understand the consequences. This can help to prevent the mistake from recurring and to find the best ways to correct it or mitigate its impact.

- **Act and implement the learning:** The final step is to apply the learning from the mistake, and make the necessary changes or adjustments. This can help to improve the situation and demonstrate the commitment and capability to learn and grow.

Examples of Successful Businesses that Have Learned from Their Mistakes

Many successful businesses have learned from their mistakes, and used them as opportunities to innovate and improve. Some examples are:

- **Apple:** In 1985, Apple fired its co-founder and visionary leader Steve Jobs, and suffered a decline in sales and reputation. However, in 1997, Apple rehired Jobs, and under his leadership, launched a series of groundbreaking products, such as the iMac, iPod, iPhone, and iPad, that revolutionized the technology industry.

- **Starbucks:** In 2008, Starbucks faced a crisis of overexpansion, declining quality, and rising competition. However, Starbucks closed hundreds of stores, retrained its baristas, and refocused on its core values of customer service and social responsibility. As a result, Starbucks regained its market share and profitability, and expanded its global presence.

- **Lego:** In the early 2000s, Lego was on the verge of bankruptcy, due to its diversification into unrelated businesses, such as video games, theme parks, and clothing. However, Lego returned to its core product of plastic bricks and leveraged its loyal fan base, digital platforms, and partnerships with popular franchises, such as Star Wars and Harry Potter, to become the world's largest toy company.

Learning from mistakes is a vital skill for businesses in today's competitive and uncertain environment. By acknowledging, analyzing, and acting on their mistakes, businesses can reap the benefits of enhanced creativity, improved performance, and increased trust and resilience. Moreover, by learning from the mistakes of others, businesses can avoid making the same errors and gain insights and inspiration from their success stories.

Fail Fast, Learn Faster

In today's competitive and dynamic business environment, organizations need to be agile, innovative, and adaptable. However, these qualities are not easy to achieve, especially when faced with uncertainty, complexity, and risk. How can businesses overcome these challenges and thrive in the market?

One possible answer is to adopt a "fail fast, learn faster" mindset. This concept, which originated in software development and project management, suggests that when trying out new ideas or solutions, it is better to test them quickly and see if they work or fail, rather than spending too much time and resources on planning, analysis, and optimization. By failing fast, businesses can identify and address problems early, reduce costs, mitigate risks, and learn from their mistakes. By learning faster, they can improve their performance, adapt to changing customer needs, and seize new opportunities.

The benefits of failing fast and learning faster are evident in many successful companies and industries. For example, Netflix, which started as a DVD rental service, quickly pivoted to online streaming when it realized that its original business model was becoming obsolete. By experimenting with different content, pricing, and delivery strategies, Netflix learned what its customers wanted and became the leader in the entertainment industry. Similarly, SpaceX, which aims to revolutionize space exploration, has embraced failure as a way to learn and innovate. By launching and testing reusable rockets, SpaceX has learned from its failures and achieved remarkable feats, such as landing a rocket on a drone ship and sending astronauts to the International Space Station.

However, failing fast and learning faster is not a simple or straightforward process. It requires a culture of experimentation, feedback, and continuous improvement, which can be challenging to create and sustain. Businesses need to overcome some common barriers, such as fear of failure, resistance to change, lack of trust, and silo mentality. To do so, they need to foster a supportive and collaborative environment where employees are encouraged to try new things, share their learnings, and learn from each other. They also need to have clear and measurable goals, metrics, and feedback mechanisms, which can help them evaluate their progress and performance. Moreover, they need to have a customer-centric approach, which can help them understand and anticipate customer needs, preferences, and behaviors.

Failing fast and learning faster is a key principle for business success in the modern world. By adopting this mindset, businesses can enhance their agility, innovation, and adaptability, and gain a competitive edge in the market. However, to implement this principle effectively, businesses need to overcome some common challenges and create a culture of experimentation, feedback, and continuous improvement. By doing so, they can not only survive, but also thrive in the face of uncertainty, complexity, and risk.

Cultivating Innovation through Failure

Innovation is the process of creating new and valuable products, services, or solutions that meet the needs of customers or society. Innovation is essential for any business that wants to survive and thrive in a competitive and dynamic market. However, innovation is not easy. It involves taking risks, experimenting, and learning from failures.

Failure is inevitable in innovation. Not every idea will work, not every prototype will succeed, and not every customer will be satisfied. Failure can be discouraging, costly, and demoralizing. But failure can also be a source of learning, improvement, and opportunity. Failure can teach us what works and what doesn't, what customers want and what they don't, what problems need to be solved, and what solutions need to be refined. Failure can also inspire us to think differently, challenge assumptions, and explore new possibilities.

Therefore, to cultivate innovation, businesses need to embrace failure as a part of the process. Businesses need to create a culture that encourages experimentation, feedback, and iteration. Businesses need to provide resources, support, and incentives for employees to try new things, learn from mistakes, and share their insights. Businesses need to celebrate failures as well as successes and reward efforts as well as outcomes.

Some examples of businesses that have cultivated innovation through failure are:

- **Google:** Google is known for its innovative products and services, such as Gmail, Google Maps, and Google Assistant. But Google also has a history of launching and shutting down many failed projects, such as Google Wave, Google Glass, and Google Plus. Google encourages its employees to spend 20% of their time on their own projects, and to test and iterate on their ideas quickly and frequently. Google also has a "fail fast, fail often" philosophy, which means that it is better to fail early and learn from it, than to invest too much time and money in something that might not work.

- **Netflix:** Netflix is the world's leading streaming service, with over 200 million subscribers and thousands of original shows and movies. But Netflix also faced many challenges and failures in its journey, such as losing customers and revenue when it tried to split its DVD and streaming businesses, facing competition from rivals like Blockbuster and Amazon, and dealing with technical issues and outages. Netflix learned from its failures and adapted its strategy, pricing, and content to meet the changing needs and preferences of its customers. Netflix also fosters a culture of innovation, where employees are empowered to make decisions, take risks, and experiment with new ideas.

- **SpaceX:** SpaceX is a pioneer in the space industry, with the vision of making humans a multi-planetary species. But SpaceX also experienced many setbacks and failures in its quest, such as losing rockets and payloads in explosions, crashes, and landing failures. SpaceX used its failures as opportunities to learn, improve, and innovate. SpaceX also embraces a culture of innovation, where employees are challenged to think big, work hard, and solve problems. SpaceX also leverages its failures to generate publicity, awareness, and support for its mission.

Failure is not the opposite of innovation, but rather a catalyst for it. By embracing failure as a part of the innovation process, businesses can learn, improve, and create new and valuable products, services, or solutions that meet the needs of customers or society.

Resilience and Growth Mindset

What makes some people succeed in business while others fail? Is it luck, talent, or something else? According to research, two of the most important factors that contribute to success are resilience and a growth mindset. These are the abilities to overcome challenges, learn from feedback, and adapt to changing situations. I will explain what resilience and growth mindset are, why they are important for business, and how to develop them.

Resilience is the capacity to recover quickly from difficulties and bounce back stronger. It is not about avoiding stress or problems, but rather facing them with courage and optimism. Resilience helps people cope with uncertainty, failure, and setbacks, which are inevitable in business. For example, a resilient entrepreneur will not give up on their idea after a rejection from an investor, but will seek another opportunity or improve their pitch. A resilient employee will not be discouraged by a negative performance review, but will use it as a chance to grow and improve.

A growth mindset is the concept that one's talents and abilities can be improved through effort and learning. It is the opposite of a fixed mindset, which assumes that one's talents are innate and fixed. A growth mindset fosters a love of learning, a willingness to take risks, and a openness to feedback. A growth mindset helps people achieve their goals and overcome challenges, which are essential for business. For example, a person with a growth mindset will not see a difficult task as a threat, but as an opportunity to learn something new. A person with a growth mindset will not avoid criticism, but will seek it as a way to improve their performance.

Resilience and growth mindset are closely related and mutually reinforcing. Resilience helps people maintain a growth mindset in the face of adversity, while a growth mindset helps people build resilience by seeing failures as learning opportunities. Together, they create a positive cycle of learning and improvement, which leads to success in business and in life.

How can one develop resilience and a growth mindset? There are several strategies that can help, such as:

- Setting realistic and challenging goals that stretch one's abilities and skills.
- Seeking feedback and learning from it, rather than taking it personally or defensively.
- Embracing challenges and difficulties as opportunities to grow and learn, rather than avoiding or fearing them.
- Celebrating successes and achievements, but also recognizing the effort and learning that went into them.
- Practicing gratitude and optimism and focusing on the positive aspects of one's situation, rather than the negative ones.
- Seeking support and guidance from others who can offer encouragement, advice, and inspiration.

Resilience and growth mindset are not fixed traits that one is born with or without. They are skills that can be learned and cultivated through practice and experience. By developing resilience and growth mindset, one can enhance their performance, productivity and satisfaction in business and in life.

Chapter 14

Knowledge Management

Knowledge management (KM) is a process of creating, storing, utilizing, and sharing knowledge within an organization. It aims to achieve organizational objectives by making the best use of knowledge. KM involves a multidisciplinary approach that draws from various fields such as business administration, information systems, management, library and information science, and others. KM can benefit an organization in many ways, such as:

Improving performance, competitive advantage, innovation, and customer satisfaction by leveraging the collective knowledge of the organization

Enhancing organizational learning and collaboration among team members, leads to faster and better decision-making.

Streamlining organizational processes, such as training and onboarding, by providing easy access to relevant and updated information.

Reducing costs and risks by avoiding duplication of efforts and preventing knowledge loss.

To implement KM effectively, an organization needs to consider three types of knowledge: tacit, implicit, and explicit. Tacit knowledge is the knowledge that is acquired through experience and intuition, and it is difficult to articulate and codify. Implicit knowledge is the knowledge that is not yet documented but can be codified with some effort. Explicit knowledge is the knowledge that is captured and stored in various formats, such as documents, databases, and reports. An organization needs to identify, organize, store, and disseminate these types of knowledge according to its needs and goals.

One of the key tools for KM is a knowledge management system (KMS), which is a system that supports the creation, storage, retrieval, and distribution of knowledge within an organization. A KMS can include various components, such as a knowledge base, a search engine, a collaboration platform, a content management system, and a learning management system. A KMS can help an organization to:

- Capture and store knowledge from various sources, such as experts, documents, and data.

- Provide easy and fast access to knowledge for users, such as employees, customers, and partners.

- Enable knowledge sharing and reuse among users, such as through forums, blogs, wikis, and social media.

- Facilitate knowledge creation and innovation, such as through feedback, ratings, and recommendations.

- Monitor and evaluate knowledge usage and quality, such as through analytics, reports, and audits.

KM is not a one-time project, but a continuous and dynamic process that requires constant adaptation and improvement. An organization needs to develop a KM strategy that aligns with its vision, mission, values, and culture. It also needs to establish a KM governance structure that defines the roles, responsibilities, and policies for KM. Moreover, it needs to foster a KM culture that encourages and rewards knowledge sharing and learning among its members. By doing so, an organization can leverage KM as a strategic asset and a source of competitive advantage.

Capturing Organizational Knowledge

Organizational knowledge is the collective wisdom, insights, and expertise that an organization possesses. It is a valuable asset that can help the organization achieve its goals, improve its performance, and gain a competitive edge. However, organizational knowledge is often tacit, meaning that it is not easily documented or communicated. It resides in the minds of employees, customers, suppliers, and other stakeholders. Therefore, capturing organizational knowledge is a challenge that requires deliberate and systematic efforts.

Capturing organizational knowledge means collecting, documenting, and storing the relevant information, experiences, and best practices within the organization. It also means making this knowledge accessible and usable for future reference, learning, and decision-making. Capturing organizational knowledge has many benefits, such as:

- **Preserving institutional memory:** Capturing organizational knowledge prevents the loss of valuable information and expertise when employees leave the organization or projects are completed. It ensures that the organization retains its history, culture, and identity.

- **Supporting decision-making:** Capturing organizational knowledge provides a foundation for informed and rational decision-making. It enables the organization to use past data, evidence, and feedback to make better choices and avoid repeating mistakes.

- **Accelerating learning:** Capturing organizational knowledge facilitates the transfer of knowledge and skills among employees. It helps new employees to quickly acquire the necessary knowledge and competencies to perform their tasks. It also encourages continuous learning and development among existing employees.

- **Promoting innovation:** Capturing organizational knowledge stimulates creativity and innovation. It allows the organization to leverage its existing knowledge to generate new ideas, solutions, and opportunities. It also encourages a culture of experimenting and learning from setbacks.

- **Enhancing collaboration:** Capturing organizational knowledge enhances collaboration and communication within and across the organization. It breaks down silos and barriers among different departments, teams, and individuals. It also enables the organization to share and exchange knowledge with external partners, such as customers, suppliers, and competitors.

To capture organizational knowledge effectively, the organization needs to adopt a strategic and systematic approach. Some of the methods and strategies that can be used are:

- **Identify knowledge sources:** The organization needs to identify the individuals, teams, and departments that have valuable knowledge and expertise relevant to its goals and objectives. It also needs to identify the external sources of knowledge, such as customers, suppliers, competitors, and industry experts.

- **Define knowledge goals:** The organization needs to clarify what specific types of knowledge it needs to capture, such as technical knowledge, customer knowledge, market knowledge, or process knowledge. It also needs to define the purpose and scope of the knowledge capture, such as for problem-solving, improvement, or innovation.

- **Choose knowledge capture tools:** The organization needs to select the appropriate tools and techniques to capture the knowledge, depending on the nature and format of the knowledge. Some of the common tools and techniques are interviews, surveys, focus groups, observations, document reviews, brainstorming, storytelling, and knowledge mapping.

- **Implement knowledge capture processes:** The organization needs to implement the knowledge capture processes in a consistent and systematic manner. It needs to ensure that the knowledge capture is aligned with the organizational goals and strategies, and that it involves the relevant stakeholders. It also needs to ensure that the knowledge capture is conducted in a timely and efficient manner, and that it follows ethical and legal standards.

- **Store and organize knowledge:** The organization needs to store and organize the captured knowledge in a secure and accessible way. It needs to use suitable knowledge management systems, such as databases, repositories, intranets, or wikis, to store the knowledge. It also needs to use appropriate knowledge classification, categorization, and indexing schemes to organize the knowledge.

- **Share and use knowledge:** The organization needs to share and use the captured knowledge for its intended purposes. It needs to disseminate the knowledge to the relevant users and stakeholders, such as employees, managers, customers, or suppliers. It also needs to apply the knowledge to support its decision-making, learning, improvement, and innovation activities.

Capturing organizational knowledge is a key to business success. It enables the organization to leverage its existing assets to achieve its goals, improve its performance, and gain a competitive edge. It also enables the organization to create a culture of knowledge-sharing, learning, and innovation. Therefore, capturing organizational knowledge should be a priority and a responsibility for every organization.

Knowledge Sharing Platforms

Knowledge is one of the most valuable assets an organization can possess in the modern era. As industries grow increasingly complex and information proliferates at an astonishing rate, the need for efficient and effective knowledge sharing becomes more pronounced. Knowledge sharing refers to the process of disseminating information, ideas, and expertise within and across organizations. It can enhance learning, problem-solving, decision-making, innovation, and performance among employees and teams. However, knowledge sharing also faces many challenges, such as information overload, silo mentality, lack of trust, and cultural barriers. Therefore, organizations need to adopt appropriate tools and strategies to facilitate and foster knowledge sharing among their members.

One of the most innovative solutions that have emerged to streamline the process of knowledge sharing is the knowledge sharing platform. A knowledge sharing platform is a centralized hub where employees can share, organize, access, and store information. It can also enable collaboration, communication, feedback, and engagement among users. A knowledge sharing platform can offer various benefits to an organization, such as:

- **Improving productivity and efficiency:** A knowledge sharing platform can help employees find and access the information they need quickly and easily, without wasting time searching through multiple sources or waiting for responses from others. This can reduce errors, duplication, and rework, and increase the quality and speed of work output.

- **Enhancing learning and development:** A knowledge sharing platform can provide employees with opportunities to learn from each other, acquire new skills, and update their knowledge. It can also support formal and informal learning initiatives, such as training, mentoring, coaching, and peer-to-peer learning.

- **Boosting innovation and creativity:** A knowledge sharing platform can stimulate the generation and exchange of new ideas, insights, and solutions among employees. It can also foster a culture of experimentation, risk-taking, and feedback, which are essential for innovation and creativity.

- **Increasing employee satisfaction and retention:** A knowledge sharing platform can improve the sense of belonging, trust, and recognition among employees. It can also empower employees to contribute, share, and grow within the organization, which can enhance their motivation, engagement, and loyalty.

To reap the benefits of a knowledge sharing platform, an organization needs to consider some key factors, such as:

- **Choosing the right platform:** An organization should select a platform that suits its needs, goals, and culture. The platform should be user-friendly, intuitive, and flexible, and it should support various file types, content formats, and search functionalities. It should also be secure, reliable, and scalable, and integrate well with other existing systems and tools.

- **Encouraging adoption and usage:** An organization should promote the awareness, understanding, and value of the platform among its employees. It should also provide adequate training, support, and incentives to encourage employees to use the platform regularly and effectively. Moreover, it should monitor and measure the usage and impact of the platform and solicit feedback and suggestions for improvement.

- **Creating and maintaining quality content:** An organization should ensure that the content on the platform is relevant, accurate, and up-to-date. It should also establish clear guidelines, standards, and processes for creating, reviewing, and updating content.

Furthermore, it should involve and empower employees to create, share, and curate content, and recognize and reward their contributions.

A knowledge-sharing platform is a powerful tool that can help an organization leverage its knowledge assets and achieve its objectives. By implementing a knowledge sharing platform, an organization can improve its productivity, efficiency, learning, development, innovation, creativity, and employee satisfaction and retention. However, to ensure the success of a knowledge sharing platform, an organization needs to choose the right platform, encourage adoption and usage, and create and maintain quality content. A knowledge-sharing platform is not a magic bullet, but a strategic investment that can yield significant returns for an organization in the long run.

Intellectual Property Protection

Intellectual property (IP) is a term that refers to the creations of the human mind, such as inventions, literary and artistic works, designs, symbols, names, and images. IP is an important asset for any business, as it can provide a competitive advantage, enhance reputation, generate revenue, and foster innovation. However, IP also needs to be protected from unauthorized use, copying, or theft by others. This is why businesses need to be aware of the different types of IP protection available and how to use them effectively.

There are four main types of IP protection: patents, trademarks, trade secrets, and copyrights.

- Patents grant the inventor the exclusive right to make, use, or sell the invention for a limited period of time, usually 20 years. Patents are useful for protecting novel, useful, and non-obvious inventions, such as machines, processes, or products. Patents can help businesses prevent competitors from copying or imitating their inventions, as well as license or sell their patents to others for profit.

- Trademarks are signs that distinguish the goods or services of one business from those of others. Trademarks can include words, logos, slogans, colors, shapes, sounds, or smells. Trademarks are valuable for building brand identity, recognition, and loyalty among customers. Trademarks can help businesses prevent confusion, deception, or dilution of their brand in the market, as well as enforce their rights against infringers or counterfeiters.

- Trade secrets are confidential information that gives a business an economic advantage over others. Trade secrets can include formulas, methods, techniques, strategies, customer lists, or data. Trade secrets are protected by keeping them secret and limiting access to them. Trade secrets can help businesses maintain their competitive edge, as well as avoid disclosure or misappropriation of their valuable information by others.

- Copyrights protect the expression of original ideas in tangible forms, such as books, music, paintings, films, or software. Copyrights grant the author the exclusive right to reproduce, distribute, perform, display, or adapt the work for a limited period of time, usually the life of the author plus 70 years. Copyrights are useful for protecting creative works, as well as generating income from royalties, licenses, or transfers.

To obtain and maintain IP protection, businesses need to follow certain steps and procedures, such as:

- Conducting IP audits to identify and evaluate their IP assets and risks
- Registering their IP rights with the relevant authorities, such as the U.S. Patent and Trademark Office (USPTO) or the World Intellectual Property Organization (WIPO)
- Monitoring and enforcing their IP rights against potential or actual infringers or violators
- Managing and exploiting their IP rights through contracts, agreements, or partnerships

IP protection is essential for any business that wants to succeed and grow in the global market. By understanding and applying the different types of IP protection, businesses can safeguard their intellectual assets, enhance their competitive advantage, and foster their innovation potential.

Data-driven Decision making

Data-driven decision-making (DDDM) is the practice of using data to guide your decision-making process and evaluate a course of action before committing to it. DDDM can help you make more confident, proactive, and cost-effective decisions in business. I will discuss the benefits of DDDM, the steps to implement it, and some examples of successful DDDM practices.

Benefits of DDDM. It has many advantages over intuition-based or opinion-based decision-making. Some of the benefits are:

DDDM can help you align your decisions with your business goals, objectives, and initiatives. By using data to measure your performance and progress, you can ensure that your actions are consistent with your desired outcomes.

DDDM can help you avoid biases and errors that may cloud your judgment. By relying on facts and evidence, you can reduce the influence of personal preferences, emotions, or assumptions that may lead you astray.

DDDM can help you improve your efficiency and effectiveness. By using data to identify problems, opportunities, and solutions, you can optimize your processes, resources, and results. You can also use data to monitor and evaluate your actions and adjust them as needed.

DDDM can help you gain a competitive edge and increase your customer satisfaction. By using data to understand your market, customers, and competitors, you can tailor your products, services, and strategies to meet their needs and expectations. You can also use data to innovate and create value for your stakeholders.

Steps to implement DDDM To implement DDDM in your business, you need to follow these steps:

- Define your business question or problem. What are you trying to achieve, solve, or improve? What are the key performance indicators (KPIs) that you will use to measure your success?

- Collect and organize your data. What data sources and methods will you use to gather the relevant information? How will you store, clean, and prepare your data for analysis?
- Analyze and interpret your data. What tools and techniques will you use to explore, visualize, and model your data? What patterns, trends, and insights can you derive from your data?

- Communicate and act on your data. How will you present and share your data findings and recommendations? How will you implement and test your data-driven decisions? How will you track and report your results and feedback?

Examples of DDDM practices Many organizations have adopted DDDM to improve their performance and outcomes. Here are some examples of DDDM practices:

- Google uses data to drive its innovation and experimentation culture. Google encourages its employees to test new ideas and products using data and analytics. Google also uses data to measure and optimize its user experience, search quality, and advertising revenue.

- Starbucks uses data to enhance its customer loyalty and personalization. Starbucks collects and analyzes data from its mobile app, loyalty program, and social media to understand its customers' preferences, behaviors, and feedback. Starbucks also uses data to customize its offers, promotions, and recommendations for its customers.

- Amazon uses data to streamline its operations and delivery. Amazon leverages data from its e-commerce platform, warehouses, and logistics network to optimize its inventory, pricing, and shipping. Amazon also uses data to predict customer demand, recommend products, and improve customer service.

DDDM is a powerful and essential process for modern business strategy. DDDM can help you make more informed, objective, and impactful decisions that align with your business goals and customer needs. To implement DDDM, you need to define your business question, collect and organize your data, analyze and interpret your data, and communicate and act on your data.

By following these steps, you can leverage the value of your data and data skills to achieve your desired outcomes.

Conclusion

The entrepreneurial journey is a dynamic and transformative experience that requires a blend of strategic foresight, resilience, continuous learning, and a passion for innovation. "Rise, Expand, Evolve, Adapt: Mastering the Journey of Entrepreneurial Success". serves as a compass for aspiring and seasoned entrepreneurs alike, offering insights into the key pillars of entrepreneurial success.

From the inception of an idea to scaling operations, navigating market changes, and embracing continuous learning, the secrets shared by seasoned entrepreneurs pave the way for sustainable growth and long-term success. The chapters on building a strong foundation, strategic growth, adaptability in the face of change, and a commitment to lifelong learning underscore the essential components of a successful entrepreneurial journey.

By unraveling the mysteries behind the success stories of successful entrepreneurs, this book not only reveals the strategies employed by industry trailblazers but also inspires readers to forge their path with confidence and determination. The blend of practical advice, real-world examples, and strategic insights equips entrepreneurs with the tools needed to overcome challenges, seize opportunities, and leave a lasting impact on the business landscape.

As the entrepreneurial landscape continues to evolve, the wisdom shared in this book serves as a timeless guide for navigating the complexities of business, fostering innovation, and building a legacy that transcends generations. With a focus on innovation, adaptability, and a growth mindset, entrepreneurs are encouraged to embark on their journey with courage, resilience, and a commitment to continuous improvement.

In essence,"Rise, Expand, Evolve, Adapt" reflects the essence of entrepreneurship—a journey filled with obstacles, victories, and vital lessons that change not just organizations but also the people behind them. This book serves as a beacon of inspiration and guidance for all those daring souls embarking on an entrepreneurial voyage. Here's to embracing the secrets of seasoned entrepreneurs and charting a course towards a future filled with success, growth, and endless possibilities.

www.ingramcontent.com/pod-product-compliance
Lightning Source LLC
Chambersburg PA
CBHW031621210526
45464CB00004B/1688